Diamond In The Rough

FIDEL DONALDSON

Diamond In The Rough

"God setteth the solitary in families: he bringeth out those which are bound with chains: but the rebellious dwell in a dry land." Psalm 68:6 (KJV)

Fidel M. Donaldson

This book is dedicated to the Christian Soldiers behind Prison Walls

Diamond In The Rough by Fidel M. Donaldson
Copyright © 2013 Appeal Ministries

ISBN: 978-09827710-2-0
LCCN: 2011960993

Cover design by: Lee Von Nutall

Editor/Book Doctor: Dr. Monica Hardy-McCray
Resumes & Beyond, Inc.
Founding President & CEO
Special thanks to Sister Gildita

Printed in the United States of America

TABLE OF CONTENTS

FOREWORD

"Where there is no understanding, there is no appreciation".
When my husband first said these words to me, I
thought, "WOW, simple, yet thought provoking".

A diamond is often referred to as a girl's best friend, but I wonder if anyone ever thought about why it's a girl's best friend. Although it is a breath taking stone, I honestly doubt it if the girl wearing the diamond even really knows why that beautiful stone that she so proudly displays has such glory and honor. Well, to me, this is no different than the anointing and destiny that God so graciously bestows upon our lives prior to existence. You see we love to brag and display beautiful, expensive things; just as we love it when God uses us in a formidable way. However, it is critical that we understand there is indeed a cost. For every carat, special cut, color and clarity there is added labor. As stated above, when we lack understanding there is no appreciation. If there is no appreciation, after one obstacle in your relationship with your spouse, you will throw the ring out the window and after one storm in your Christian life; you will backslide and turn from God.

Not picking on the ladies, as I am one that loves nice things myself, but how many times have a woman been offended by a small, eloquent diamond versus a large rock when the person giving the diamond has worked tirelessly to obtain it? Moreover, how many Christians would rather attend a prophetic conference "to get a word from a prophet", versus making a sacrifice of fasting, praying and lying before the Lord themselves for that same word? Many times we want to reap the benefits of someone else's labor not understanding that there is a painstaking story behind the glory.

In this book, Apostle Fidel serves as a Mineworker; he puts on a hard hat and goes down into the earth of his soul to dig out what appears to be chunks of carbon then begins to apply HEATED biblical truths to them so you can BECOME the diamond God destined you to be. Mining is dirty and it is labor intensive, it can also be dangerous depending on what type of mining is being done. The world is like a diamond mine and sinners are the rough diamonds, bound, waiting to be mined, cut and polished. Apostle Fidel is not only mining for diamonds in the rough, he is showing all born again, spirit-filled believers how to become miners. This book is indeed a page turner, but I challenge you to turn the pages slowly as it is packed with word and prophetic impartations that will quicken your spirit to repent, pray and even grab your bible for further study. This book is powerful; it WILL cut you! As I read this book, it forced me to examine myself, which means I had to look closer at my motives, my stamina and my fruit; yes, all nine virtues of God.

Apostle Fidel has an unbelievable testimony, he is an end-time, anointed vessel of God called to teach, preach and speak into the hearts of ALL God's people. No matter where you are geographically, physically, spiritually, emotionally, socially, financially, psychologically, interpersonally or organizationally; this man of God has a word to meet you right where you are. This book was written to equip you and to provide you with the proper tools to function as true disciples of God so you won't fall for distractions or illusions, which impair your discernment to a point where you think a cubic zirconium is a diamond.

Dr. Monica Hardy-McCray
The Tabernacle International Deliverance Ministry
Co-Founder & Pastor

PREFACE

*T*he phrase diamond in the rough is a metaphor for the original unpolished state of diamond gemstones, especially those that have the potential to become high quality jewels. Born again believers in the Lord Jesus Christ are like rough diamonds in need of cutting and polishing. They have the potential to be priceless stones but need to endure the process of His cutting and polishing tools. Diamonds do not start out as valuable and beautiful gem stones. They have to go through a natural process to attain their value, beauty, and sturdiness. Believers who yield themselves to Jesus Christ through the Holy Ghost will go through a supernatural process of transformation to go from a diamond in the rough to a priceless brilliant cut diamond.

Atoms of carbon must go through a long intense process of intense heat and pressure in the earth's mantle to become a rough diamond. Once the diamond is brought to the earth's surface it has to be mined, then a gemologist has to cut and polish it in-order to prepare it to be showcased in the window of a jewelry store. The life of the believer in Jesus Christ has to go through a process of intense heat and pressure in the furnace of affliction so the light of His glory can shine in and through them. The more intense the heat and pressure the more the light will shine. The heat and pressure is necessary to remove all of the trash that was picked up in the world when the believer lived according to the rules of the carnal mind.

Quality diamonds are rare and expensive because many diamonds which are unearthed are estimated to be more than three billion years old. We live in a microwave society where we desire to have things now. There are times when I place my food in the microwave and because I am hungry and anxious to eat, I pull it out before the end of the allotted heating time. Once the food is taken out, I start eating only to discover that the top is hot but the middle is cold. God does not employ the microwave process when dealing with the life of a convert; He employs the rotisserie process. He keeps us over the fire slow roasting until every thought, word and deed in us that does not bring glory to Him dissolves and burns in the fire. God's heat and pressure takes the believer through a purifying process in preparation to carry His glory.

The glory of God will not dwell in a carnal place; His plan is to have a people who can carry His glory in the earth. Diamonds are one of the hardest if not the hardest substance known to man. The process of extreme heat and pressure is what gives them their toughness and that toughness allows them to cut steel. The disciples of the Lord Jesus Christ must attain a level of toughness to carry God's glory, which are His weight and His splendor. The radiant diamond glistens in the showroom window because it has endured a process. The disciple is God's diamond and he must endure God's process to be called a son of God. God's sons will alleviate creation from its groaning so they must be battled tested in the furnace until His will and desire is formed in them.

PART ONE

Chapter 1
Rock of Ages

If you understood where I came from, you would appreciate where God is taking me; from rock to diamond

*D*iamonds originated deep within the earth as simple atoms of carbon. The carbon is compressed into a rock and carried to the earth's surface by volcanic magma eruptions. Unlike any diamond made by man, Jesus is the solid Rock, the son of the Almighty God, the Word that was made flesh. He is seated at the right hand of God making intercession for His body, but he had to go through a process before He was highly exalted by God our Father and given a name that is above every name. *"Though he were a Son, yet learned he obedience by the things which he suffered; And being made perfect, he became the author of eternal salvation unto all them that obey him; Called of God an high priest after the order of Melchisedec" Hebrews 5:8-10(KJV).*

Jesus did not have to be born again to become a son. From the time He was conceived in His mother's womb He was the Son of God. The angel Gabriel told Mary that the Holy Ghost would come upon her, and the power of the Highest would overshadow her. The angel went on to say, *"Therefore also that holy thing which shall be born of thee shall be called the Son of God" Luke 1:35 (KJV).* Jesus was born holy but he had to go through the process of suffering to be able to bear our infirmities, and carry our sins on the cross. He was born Jesus but was made Lord and Christ. He was made Lord and Christ through suffering. In his sermon on the day of Pentecost the Apostle Peter told his audience, *"Therefore let all the house of Israel know assuredly, that God hath made that same Jesus whom ye have crucified both Lord and Christ" Acts 2:36 (KJV).* He grew up as the carpenter's son but God used the cross to make Him Lord and Christ.

If He is to be Lord and Christ in our lives then we must bear our cross. The song writer declared, *"Must Jesus bear the cross alone while all the world goes free?"* He bore the cross for the sin of the world and we must bear the cross of self-denial. Jesus declared, *"if any man will come after me, let him deny himself, and take up his cross, and follow me" Matthew 16:24(KJV).* Self-denial is not a natural concept for us because we are pacified when we come into this world as babies. Our carnal natures want anything but self-denial; on the contrary, it wants to be the center of attention. For this reason, we have to lose our carnal minds and take on the mind of Jesus Christ. His mind is geared towards accomplishing the will of God the Father. If we are to accomplish the will of God then our carnal minds must be nailed to the cross.

The Apostle Paul declared, *"I am crucified with Christ: nevertheless I live; yet not I, but Christ liveth in me: and the life which I now live in the flesh I live by the faith of the Son of God, who loved me, and gave himself for me" Galatians 2:20(KJV).* We understand that Paul did not hang on the cross with or next to Jesus like the two thieves. He is referring to the Adamic nature, the old man who was controlled by sin; that man was crucified with Christ so the new man could live through faith in Christ. Paul mentions the fact that Christ gave Himself for him because He loved him. What an awesome revelation of the depth of God's love for us. He sent His only begotten son as a love gift for us when we deserved to die. Our Father in heaven is not a condemning God He is a loving Father. People who are running around strapping bombs to themselves in an effort to kill and maim, need to get a true revelation of Father God. He has a loving heart and does not take any delight in the death of the wicked.

The true and living God is looking to restore; not to destroy. Unrepentant sin brings condemnation and death, but God sent His son to take death for us. Like the atoms of carbon, which are compressed in the earth to become a rock, which will become a diamond; His body was compressed in the garden of Gethsemane, beaten and battered then hung up on a cross. He never suffered for Himself because He is holy. Everything that He suffered was for future sons. *"For he hath made him to be sin for us, who knew no sin; that we might be made the righteousness of God in him" 2 Corinthians 5:21(KJV).* Can you imagine the amount of sin He had to bear, the sin of all people, past, present and future; it is mind boggling and almost inconceivable.

Although He was without sin, He went through the process of being made perfect. If Jesus had to go through the process of suffering to learn obedience, we must understand that we cannot attain sonship without suffering? We will not be made perfect without suffering. Peter declared, *"Forasmuch then as Christ hath suffered for us in the flesh, arm yourselves likewise with the same mind: for he that hath suffered in the flesh hath ceased from sin" 1 Peter 4:1(KJV).* It would be nice if we could learn obedience in a comfortable classroom, but it appears that our greatest lessons in life are learned through the things we suffer. Life's most important lessons are not learned when things are going well, because we maintain the status quo when there are no challenges. It is God's love and kindness that draws a sinner to Him, but the sinner normally does not receive that love and kindness until his back is against the wall because some calamity has befallen him.

Solitary Confinement: Encountering the Rock

I can definitely speak for myself when it comes to tragedy leading an individual to repent and cry out to God. Prior to coming to salvation through Jesus Christ; I heard the gospel preached many times but refused to repent. The sinner always believes he has more time. My life was totally consumed with the pleasures of sin. It was carnality for breakfast, lunch and dinner. The occasional times I did darken the door steps of a church were on a religious holiday like Easter, or if I was invited to a baby's christening. I smuggled drugs, fornicated, drank and did other sinful things in a futile attempt to satisfy the insatiable appetite of my flesh, all to no avail because the flesh always requires more.

When you are in the world and you are looking to have fun, you will travel far and wide, and spend as much as necessary. If you go to a night club or a party one weekend, the flesh will want a better one the next time. If you find a nice looking female or male to get your groove on with, the flesh will want a prettier, sexier one the next time. If getting high was the way you tried to satisfy the flesh, you looked for the best high you could get. I was told that people who get hooked on crack get such an overjoyed sensation on the first hit; they are willing to spend a great deal of time and finances chasing that high. Their pursuit of that pleasurable moment is so intense they will stop eating; taking showers, hang on street corners and in crack houses like zombies while searching for the next hit.

I was so consumed with sin that I could not see that my life was headed in a dangerous direction. Reality hit me when I was arrested in South London in a house and charged with conspiracy to smuggle and distribute cocaine. I will never forget the day they took me to a prison called Wormwood-Scrubs in London and placed me on 23-hours a day lock down in a cell without a toilet. When you wind up in a situation like that, you will get a revelation real fast that it is not all about you. I was far removed from the Moet champagne I drank in the night clubs, far removed from the expensive clothing and sweet smelling cologne I wore, far removed from the party girls I ran around with when I should have been home helping my wife by being a good husband and father.

Sin will take you farther than you want to go, keep you longer than you want to stay and cost you more than you want to pay. When I looked around I realized I was in a pen with no hens, just a bunch of roosters; I saw a lot of bulls and asked where are the heifers? At that moment, I knew it would be my last time being in prison. I was facing a long prison sentence in England, and the situation was worsened when I found out there was an attempt being made to indict me in the Midwest for being part of an organized drug gang. I did not need anyone to tell me that my life needed an immediate change.

Prior to my arrest I was a *"Mister Know It All"* who thought I did not have to listen to wise counsel from others. I was a fast talker who did not know that my mouth was writing checks my behind could not or would not be able to cash. Being in a cell with another inmate without a toilet in the cell was very humbling. I was not known for my humility when I was free so I ended up in a solitary place; far away from the dimly lit dance halls, discos and house parties, the fast money drugs, the fast flowing alcoholic beverages, and the flashing night club lights that added to the ambiance and the mystique. So far from the curvaceous members of the opposite sex who drew me because of the lust of my eyes.

Although I was surrounded by guards and other criminals, I sat alone in that prison. It is amazing how a person can be in a crowd and still feel lonely. I longed for my precious wife and the children I was too busy to spend time with because of my lascivious and lustful lifestyle. I thank God that He is the God of another chance. Many people know Him as the God of a second chance, but I had used up my second chance a long time ago. Once day I found a Gideon New Testament Bible in the cell and began to read it. When my wife used to ask me to go to church with her, my response was, get out of here with that white man's religion, fools go to church on Sunday. My epiphany came when I read the book of John.

In this Gospel, John records an incident where some religious folks tried to kill Jesus because He healed a man on the Sabbath at a pool called Bethesda. Jesus told them to *"Search the scriptures; for in them ye think ye have eternal life: and they are they which testify of me. And ye will not come to me, that ye might have life John 5:39-40(KJV).* I heard the voice of Jesus calling me to repentance so I bowed my knees in my cell and asked Him to forgive me of my sins and be the Lord of my life. It was March 6, 1991, and I remember it as if it was today. It was a watershed moment and an epiphany for me. When He came into my heart and forgave my sins I knew it was not jail house religion but a true conversion because I began to witness of His goodness and mercy to other inmates immediately. I know the power that is in the name of the Lord Jesus to deliver a wretched sinner, because He delivered me.

At the end of one year on remand, I was sentenced to eight years, and sent to a prison called the Isle of Sheppy. The prison was next to a pig's farm and the stench of the hogs used to fill my cell when the wind blew. I found out from a fellow inmate that the oatmeal I ate for breakfast had pig's meal stamped on the bags. The prodigal son in the Bible desired to fill his belly with the husks that the swine ate; I was actually eating the oatmeal that was used to fatten the pigs. When I arrived and was escorted to the landing where I would spend the next couple of years, I noticed most of the inmates on the landing were doing life sentences.

Fortunately, I had peace because my life was transformed by the encounter I had with King Jesus in my cell before I arrived on the Isle of Sheppy. As stated in *Romans 12:2*, because my mind was renewed I was a transformed person despite the fact I was physically in the same place as the other inmates. I did not miss the flashy lifestyle I lived as an international drug smuggler. The paranoia of the destructive lifestyle was replaced by the peace of God which passes all understanding. I had peace because I knew Jesus would be with me throughout the sentence. I really did not know how much time I would have to spend in prison, but I knew I got His word in me before I left England because I could not return home with the same mindset that I left. I was a new creature in Christ, but that creature was an infant who first needed the milk of His word before he could start eating meat. Many people have a genuine encounter with Jesus but fall by the wayside because they do not build on the foundation He places in them. I was committed to living my life for Christ in the prison and when I was released.

I was committed to being the best husband and father I could be, and the way to do both was to fill myself with His word and to live by its principles. David declared, *"thy word have I hid in mine heart, that I might not sin against thee. Thy word is a lamp unto my feet and a light unto my path" Psalm 119:11, 105(KJV).* I developed an insatiable appetite to learn about God, so I began to study day and night. While other inmates were brewing hooch (akin to moonshine, which is a crude unrefined form of alcohol), sticking hashish, marijuana, and other illicit drugs up their buts to smuggle them into the prison; I went around witnessing the gospel of Jesus Christ. I eventually started a Bible study group in my cell and my diligent study of His word brought illumination to my spiritually darkened mind.   As I studied His word I received the revelation of how He used my incarceration and the solitary environment of my cell to build a foundation in me. Bethesda means house of mercy; it had five porches and five is the number of grace. My eight year sentence represented a new spiritual beginning in my life because eight represents new beginnings.   God used grace and mercy to give me a new beginning in Jesus Christ. Hallelujah!!

I am totally convinced that if it were not for my incarceration I probably would have died a horrible death pursuing a life of crime, or wound up with a life sentence. I learned obedience through the suffering I endured when I lost my freedom, and I thank God for it because without it I know I would have missed the precious gift of salvation. If sin has led you to a place of suffering and you are reading this right now, you can receive your deliverance just like I did by calling on the name of Jesus. You do not have to die in your condition; repent (recognize the wrong in your life and be truly sorry about it) and start your new life in Christ Jesus today.

Jesus is the solid Rock and He desires to save you and to use you mightily, but the process begins with your willingness to repent and surrender your heart to Him. There is no sin you have committed that the Blood of Jesus cannot cleanse. There is no hole that is so deep that He cannot reach down and pull you out. His arms are outstretched waiting to receive you as a son of God. Repentance is the bridge that leads you to Him. If you are building your life on anything besides Jesus Christ the solid Rock, your life will not be able to withstand the storms that are ahead.

Jesus tells us in the word that the wise man built his house on the rock and when the rains, the floods, and the winds came and beat on it, the house was able to stand because it was founded upon a rock. The house is the disciple and Jesus is the rock upon which the disciple is built. The rains, the floods, and the winds represent the suffering the disciple has to endure to be made perfect and become a son. The reason why the house will not fall is because Jesus endured every form of suffering and temptation a disciple will ever face and He never fell. *"For we have not an high priest which cannot be touched with the feeling of our infirmities; but was in all points tempted like as we are, yet without sin" Hebrews 4:15(KJV).*

There is no temptation that can come to us that Jesus did not face and overcome. We succumb at times but we must never allow ourselves to walk in a spirit of condemnation because repentance and restoration is just a prayer and a confession away. We go through the process of suffering for sonship because at some point we are expected to come to a level of maturity where God can empower us and use us as His ambassadors of the gospel. Without the preparation which comes through suffering the disciple will not be able to withstand the demonic attacks they will invariably suffer as they advance the kingdom of God. Jesus came unto His own and His own received Him not, *but as many as received Him, to them He gave power to become the sons of God, even to them that believe on His name; which were born, not of blood, nor of the will of the flesh, nor of the will of man, but of God John 1:12-13(KJV).* Jesus Christ is the solid Rock, the Rock of ages and we must be compressed so the solid Rock can be formed in us. Remember, the atoms of carbon have to go through a process of compression through intense heat and pressure to become a diamond forming rock. The heat and pressure you are feeling at the present time are the forces God is using to compress you into a rock forming diamond by allowing Christ the solid Rock to be formed.

The Apostle Paul travailed in birth on several occasion for the Galatians. The first travail was for their salvation, and then he travailed so Christ could be formed in them. The Greek word for form is, *morphoo, it means to fashion*; it comes from the root word *morphe (pronounced mor-fay)* which means to adjust or shape the nature. Paul's desire for the Galatians was that they take on the form or the image of Christ. This is the desire of God for all His children, that His Son live in and through them. We must endeavor to press beyond the dictates and confines of religion into a life transforming relationship with our Lord. Salvation is not an end in itself, but a means to an end. God did not send Jesus to die on the cross for our sins so we can sit on church benches or chairs waiting for the rapture. God has a nobler purpose than that. Salvation is our starting point on a great journey. The journey must take us beyond denominationalism.

God told Jeremiah to, *"Arise, and go down to the potter's house, and there I will cause thee to hear my words" (Jeremiah 18:2).* When Jeremiah arrived the potter wrought a work on the wheels. There was a clay vessel in the hand of the potter and it was marred. The Hebrew word for marred is *shachath (pronounced shaw-khath)* and it means to decay, to ruin or to cast off. God is the potter and we are the clay whose vessels are marred with sin. Our carnal natures are corrupt and in ruins so God has to destroy it so our vessels can be cleansed. God worked the marred vessel into another vessel because He is a loving and merciful God. He could have cast the marred vessel into the trash, but He kept it on the wheel until it turned into a vessel that was good to Him.

Beloved, allow the potter to keep you on the wheel until He sees another vessel that is pleasing to Him. The vessel that is pleasing to Him is the one in which Christ can dwell. Prior to salvation our vessels were a temple for demons. Christ shed His blood so our vessels could be cleansed, and used a dwelling place for the Holy Spirit. The potter's wheel is not pleasant to the flesh but it is necessary for the transformation process. On the potter's wheel our wills are broken so His will can be formed in us. It is important not try to get off the wheel before the new vessel is completed. When flesh is screaming to get off, allow God's grace, mercy and love to strengthen you. The vessel has to be strong enough to contain the Rock.

Rock or Sand?

Jesus compared those who heard and acted upon His sayings as a wise man which built his house upon a rock, and those who failed to act upon His sayings as a foolish man which built his house upon sand. It is hard to imagine anyone building their house upon sand, so we must examine Jesus' sayings in context. Anyone whose life is not built on Christ the solid Rock has a house with a foundation made of sand. A house of that sort may stand for a while but at some point it will fall from the onslaught of the rain, the floods, and the winds. Through the ages men have tried to build their houses on wealth, prestige, and fame, but in times of trouble, those foundations gave way because they were not firm enough to hold the weight of the house. Have you ever been to the beach and saw a sand castle being built? It looks cool when it is finished but as soon as a gust of wind or some wave hit it, it began to disintegrate; so it is with the person's life that is not built on Christ.

None of the religious belief systems in the world are the proper foundation. I am sure most if not all of them have some truth to them but Jesus said, *"I am the way, the truth, and the life: no man cometh to the Father, but by me" John 14:6(KJV)*. Why settle for something that has some truth when you can have the truth. Since Jesus is the truth then all religions are false, even if they have some truth in them. Since Jesus is the way then the religions of this world will not lead us to the Father. Since Jesus is the life then the religions of this world will not be able to give us spiritual life. I know in this politically correct world people want us to co-exist and pray together under the umbrella of spiritual ecumenism, but Jesus makes it clear as recorded in *John 14:6,* He is the only way to the Father; He is the only truth and the life. Jesus is the narrow road which leads us to eternal life; all other roads are broad roads which lead to destruction. Few find the narrow road but many are traveling on the wide deceptive road of destruction. No matter how much persecution we have to endure, we must not compromise our faith in Christ alone.

A Revelation of the Rock

The disciples who traveled with Jesus received a revelation of the Rock upon which we are being built. When they traveled with Him to the coast of Caesarea Philippi, He asked the disciples who the people thought He was. It was there that Peter received the revelation from the Father that Jesus was the Christ, the Son of the Living God. *"And Jesus answered and said unto him, Blessed art thou, Simon Barjona: for flesh and blood hath not revealed it unto thee, but my Father which is in heaven. And I say also unto thee, That thou art Peter, and upon this rock I will build my church; and the gates of hell shall not prevail against it. Matthew 16:17-18(KJV).*

The Greek word for revealed as it is used in Matthew 16:17 is *apokalupto* (pronounced *ap-ok-al-oop-to*) and it means, to take the cover off or to disclose. Simon Peter and the other disciples were blessed because of the revelation they received from the Father. True revelation comes from the Father of lights, not from flesh and blood. It does not matter how charismatic the preacher is, how well he dots the "I" and crosses the "T", he cannot bring forth Holy Spirit revelation unless the Father gives it to him. At that pivotal moment in the coast of Caesarea Philippi, God not only disclosed the identity of Jesus as the Christ, the Son of the living God, but the revelation of the building of the church was disclosed. Jesus was not referring to a temple made with human hands but an *ekklesia*. This is the Greek word for church and it means a calling out, an assembly. It comes from the word *ek* which means out and *kaleo* which means to call.

The church of the Lord Jesus Christ is made up of individuals who have received and embraced the revelation that Jesus is the Christ, the Son of the living God. The revelation of Jesus' sonship and the fact that He is the Messiah spoken of by the Old Testament prophets is the bedrock and foundation of every true believer. The church is not being built on the Pope of Rome, past, present or future. Millions of people all over the world have been told that Peter was the first pope and the church is being built on Peter and all the popes who have succeeded him. My question to you the reader is where is the scriptural evidence for this claim? The Rock has to be the revelation and not Peter because the revelation is; Jesus is the Christ, the Son of the living God. That is the only foundation, the only rock that can hold the colossal structure being built by our Lord and Savior.

The Formation of a Rock

A good gemologist has trained eyes which can spot a fake diamond; a demon can spot a carnal Christian who has not been tried in the fire with ease. The more intense the heat and pressure, the greater the ability to stand; our ability to stand is critical because we must have a firm foundation in Christ if God is to use us to bring out those who are bound with chains. Demons will not relinquish their authority, jurisdiction, and influence over individuals who are bound without a fight. When we learn to suffer with Christ then we will be qualified to reign with Him. The Apostle Paul declared, *"For I reckon that the sufferings of this present time are not worthy to be compared with the glory which shall be revealed in us" Romans 8:18(KJV).* Whatever the present suffering you are enduring, keep in mind, you are *a diamond in the rough*, and the suffering is the rough that is forming the diamond in you.

If we could carry His glory without suffering then everyone who says Lord, Lord would have the glory. His glory speaks of His weight and His splendor. To have the weight and splendor of a glorious diamond we must endure the heat and pressure of the furnace; there is no way around it. Anyone can shout when the battle is over and victory is won, but who can shout in the midst of the battle? Who can shout when their home is about to be auctioned off because of foreclosure? Who can shout when a pink slip is received and bills are piling up? Who can shout in the midst of loneliness brought about by divorce or the death of a loved one?

The one who can shout in the midst of the heat and pressure will be counted worthy to carry His glory, because the glory tells the story. I heard a preacher once say, *"You see the glory but you don't know the story."* I may not know the particulars of the story, but the level of glory tells me the depth of the story. Take your eyes off the process of compression, off the heat and pressure and focus on the glory which shall be revealed in you. The three Hebrew boys told King Nebuchadnezzar their God could deliver them but if He did not they would not bow down to his idol. Hold your head up and shout on to God with the voice of triumph. The enemy wants you to bow in the midst of the heat and pressure, but confound him by giving God thanks for allowing you to be formed like a chain cutting diamond through the pressure.

God has given us, authority, jurisdiction, and delegated influence over the demonic realm. Your level of authority, jurisdiction and delegated influence is correlated to your level of heat and pressure compression. As foresaid Demons and the kingdom or darkness will not roll over and play dead as we advance the kingdom of God. We are locked in a war against the forces of darkness and that is the reason we had to and have to be compressed into a rock like the carbon atom in the earth. The kingdom of God is advanced when a sinner comes out of darkness into the marvelous light of the Lord Jesus. When the sinner is delivered from darkness by grace through faith in the Lord Jesus; he is positioned to receive the promise of the Spirit which is the blessing God promised Abraham He would give to the families of the earth.

This war requires frontline warriors so soldiers need not enlist. When David's family and the family of the men who traveled with him were taken captive by the Amalekites, when Ziklag was burned with fire and the people spoke of stoning David; he had no time to have a pity party over his possessions. He sent for the ephod and asked the LORD if he should pursue, and was he going to overtake them, and the LORD said, *"pursue: for thou shalt surely overtake them, and without fail recover all" 2 Samuel 30:8(KJV).* David had six hundred men with him when he came to the brook Besor, but only four hundred were able to cross the brook because the other two hundred were too faint. Are you going to be a part of the four hundred who cross over in pursuit of the possessions stolen by the enemy or will you be part of the two hundred too faint to cross over? Your present suffering is what will give you the strength to cross over if you do not faint. *"And let us not be weary in well doing: for in due season we shall reap, if we faint not" Galatians 6:9(KJV).*

When we are in spiritual warfare it is imperative we understand where the weak links are in our army and leave them behind. Many believers are carrying dead weight with them into battle and wonder why they are not victorious. Do not allow your emotions to cloud your decision making process. If David had felt sorry for the fain and tried to carry them into the battle, they would have slowed his pursuit. David was able to overtake the enemy and recover all because he left the two hundred faint men behind. We cannot take insufficient things in battle and expect to gain victory. God's plan is for us to have complete victory; like Christ we will have to endure suffering so God can complete His work in us and make us sons.

Paul told the church at Rome that creation is groaning, waiting for the manifestation of the sons of God. In order for the sons of God to alleviate creation from its groaning they must be empowered by Gods Holy Spirit. The Spirit of God will not dwell in defiled polluted temples so He takes His disciple through the process of learning obedience through suffering so the disciple can be perfected like Jesus Christ. We have many believers in the world who acknowledge Jesus as savior, but the sons of God acknowledge Him as Lord and Savior. Sons are willing to submit to His Lordship. They understand that they have to die to everything that is carnal and fleshly so they can walk in the power of the Spirit.

Chapter 2
Diamond Characteristics

Knowing who you are will keep others from misidentifying you

*D*iamonds are described using 4 C's: Cut, Clarity, Color and Carat. **Cut:** is a diamond's most important characteristic. It has the greatest overall influence on a diamond's beauty. It determines what we generally think of when we hear the word sparkle. Research suggests that diamond cutting is the art, skill and increasingly science of changing a diamond from a rough stone into a faceted gem. Cutting diamond requires specialized knowledge, tools, equipment, and techniques because of its extreme difficulty.

The first guild of diamond cutters and polishers (Diamantaire) was formed in 1375 in Nuremberg, Germany, and led to the development of various types of 'Cut'. Diamonds have two distinct meanings when it comes down to 'cut'. The first meaning to cut refers to the shape: square, princess, oval, round, heart, marquise, pear, etc. The second meaning to cut relates to the specific quality of cut within the shape; the quality and price will vary greatly based on the cut quality. Since diamonds are very hard to cut, special diamond-bladed edges are used to cut them. The first major development in diamond cutting came with the "Point Cut". The Point Cut follows the natural shape of an octahedral raw diamond crystal, which eliminates waste in the cutting process.

Even with modern techniques, the cutting and polishing of a diamond crystal always results in a dramatic loss of weight (i.e., about 50%). Sometimes the cutters compromise and accept lesser proportions and symmetry in order to avoid inclusions or to preserve the weight. Since the per-carat price of a diamond shifts around key milestones (such as 1.00 carat), many one-carat (200 mg) diamonds are the result of compromising; in other words, they cut the quality for Carat weight. Some jewelry experts advise consumers to buy a 0.99 carat (198 mg) diamond for its better price or buy a 1.10 carat (220 mg) diamond for its better cut, avoiding a 1.00 carat (200 mg) diamond, which is more likely to be a poorly cut stone.

The level of skill of the stone cutter will determine what type of diamond is brought forth. The quality of cut not only determines the shape but the price of the diamond. The cutter carefully examines the crystal of the gemstone to determine how much of the crystal should be cut away to produce a stone or stones with good clarity. The cutter must determine which stone shapes will make maximum use of the crystal. The cutter must make as much use of the crystal as he can, as a diamond is too valuable to waste. To achieve an ideal stone, the cutter must cut to mathematical specifications to allow a maximum amount of light to be reflected through the stone. This type of cut is known as the Brilliant cut. It is important that the diamond is cut neither too much nor too little, as the purpose of the best cut is to produce a diamond with brilliance and fire characteristics.

After carefully studying the cut of the diamond it is no question that our Father in heaven is the master cutter. Through His omniscience; He has the expertise necessary to ascertain the best angle to position His chosen vessels so they can be cut to the specific proportions and dimensions, which gives the greatest pathway of light. Because of His expertise, He does not have to compromise and accept lesser proportions and symmetry in order to avoid inclusions or to preserve the weight. The weight we lose on His cutting table is the junk of the flesh that weighs us down, keeping us from soaring to greater dimensions of His glory. His precision cuts allow us to get to a place where we can carry the weight and splendor of His glory.

Inclusion and compromise will not be tolerated by Him; 0.99% is not acceptable to Him. His cut has to be precise because His gem will be priceless. Cutting can influence the color grade of a diamond, thereby raising its value. Certain cut shapes are used to intensify the color of the diamond. The radiant cut is an example of this type of cut. Natural green color diamonds most often have merely a surface coloration caused by natural irradiation, which does not extend through the stone. For this reason green diamonds are cut with significant portions of the original rough diamonds surface (naturals) left on the finished gem. It is these naturals that provide the color to the diamond. Inclusion and compromise also affects color and value. As His chosen vessels, and His diamond we must radiate with His glory, by having the color of the glorified body of the Lord Jesus. The Apostle John gives us a picture of Him, *"And I turned to see the voice that spake with me. And being turned, I saw seven golden candlesticks; And in the midst of the seven candlesticks one like unto the Son of man, clothed with a garment down to the foot, and girt about the paps with a golden girdle. His head and his hairs were white like wool, as white as snow; and his eyes were as a flame of fire; And his feet like unto fine brass, as if they burned in a furnace; and his voice as the sound of many waters"* Revelation 1:12-15(KJV).

Sharper Than Any Two Edged Sword

The cutting tool used by our Father is the word. *"For the word of God is quick, and powerful, and sharper than any two-edged sword, piercing even to the dividing asunder of soul and spirit, and of the joints and marrow, and is a discerner of the thoughts and intents of the heart"* Hebrews 4:12(KJV). As foresaid, the value of the diamond is dependent on the cut. It is wonderful to know that our heavenly Father the Gemologist and master stone cutter, is the one in charge of cutting and polishing us. God's word has the ability to cut through the things in our hearts and minds that keep us from reflecting the light of Jesus Christ. All we have to do is keep ourselves on the Altar, which is His cutting table, and be willing to let the word do the work. A beautiful diamond cannot be produced without cutting and polishing; a beautiful disciple reflecting the light of Jesus cannot be produced without being cut and polished by the Master cutter. The rough diamond that does not go through this process looks dull and has jagged edges; it cannot be compared to the lovely diamonds seen in jewelry cases.

A Real Life, Diamond Cut Story

In July 2011, I was diagnosed with a massive meningioma tumor. The tumor was located in my head behind my right eye. After being examined by several physicians, neurologists, ophthalmologists and oncologists; and undergoing numerous CT scans and MRIs; it was determined that surgery was the best option to remove the massive tumor and stop the growth. What should have been a three hour surgical procedure, took almost seven hours to complete. I was later told that because of the size and location of the tumor, and the massive damage the meningioma had done to the bone of my skull; that the regular drill bits normally used would not cut through the damaged skull. Finally, the doctors had to use a **"Diamond bit drill"** to **"Cut"** and remove a fourth of my skull. After surgery, the doctor pulled my husband aside to explain why the procedure took so long. He told him that the regular drill bit kept breaking because of the condition of my skull. My husband replied, "Doctor I told you she was Hard-Headed". The doctor then told him that the prostatic skull was held in place by several titanium screws. When my husband heard that, he said to the doctor, "So now I can honestly say, honey you have a few screws loose". While we had the joy and pleasure of laughing at my expense, I had a few replies of my own. I told them, "First of all, when GOD made me, He only used the best material - not cheap stuff. He made me a strong woman and not a weak woman". "Second, **it takes a Diamond to cut a Diamond**"; after all, Diamonds are a Girl's Best Friend! Today I am proud to tell my story and testify that the tumor was removed successfully. Thanks be to GOD, I am Healed, Healthy & Whole! From this ordeal, Diamond Cut Women's Ministries was born. I was given the mandate by GOD to minister to all of His Precious daughters that are indeed precious Diamonds!

Pastor Karen Muse
Diamond Cut Women Ministries
He brought me through the "Gory"
so I can tell the "Story"-To God be all the "Glory"!

As demonstrated in the story referenced above, a diamond blade is tough enough to cut steel, so the word of God is tough enough to cut through any steel fortress or strongholds that have been erected in our flesh. The same word that cuts also polishes us and prepares us for display. The cutting process is not easy to bear but when we focus on the brilliance that will ensue, we gain the strength to endure the seasons of cutting. Despite the pain that is associated with the cutting process let's examine exactly what is taking place:

1. **Ideal cut:** Represents roughly the top 3% of diamond quality based on cut; Reflects nearly all light that enters the diamond; an exquisite and rare cut.
2. **Very good cut:** Represents roughly the top 15% of diamond quality based on cut; reflects nearly as much light as the ideal cut, but for a lower price.
3. **Good cut:** Represents roughly the top 25% of diamond quality based on cut; Reflects most light that enters; much less expensive than a very good cut.
4. **Fair cut:** Represents roughly the top 35% of diamond quality based on cut. Still a quality diamond, but a fair cut will not be as brilliant as a good cut.
5. **Poor cut:** Diamonds that are generally so deep and narrow or shallow and wide lose most of the light out the sides and bottom.

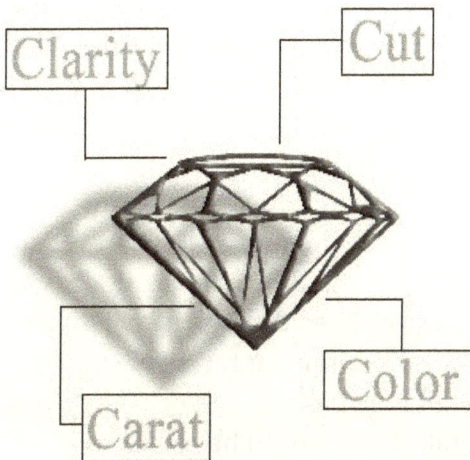

Once the diamond is cut it will go through the process of polishing to obtain a smooth surface; it is at this time a diamond receives its classification according to the last **3 C's:**

Clarity: is the easiest to understand, and according to many experts, generally has the least impact on a diamond's appearance. Clarity simply refers to the tiny, natural imperfections that occur in all but the finest diamonds. Gemologists refer to these imperfections by a variety of technical names, including blemishes and inclusions, among others. Diamonds with the least and smallest imperfections receive the highest clarity grades. Because these imperfections tend to be microscopic, they do not generally affect a diamond's beauty in any discernible way.

Carat: is a measure of a diamond's weight. To fully understand the size of a diamond, carat weight should be considered in conjunction with two other criteria: distance in millimeters across the top of the diamond and the diamond's cut grade.

Color: is used to describe the color present within a diamond or gemstone. These colors have been established by expert gemological laboratories, and are carefully scrutinized against a master set of diamonds. For diamonds, the color range starts from D which represents the whitest diamond to Z, which represents the yellowish color in the spectrum range. The white is considered to be the rarest diamond color. The color of a diamond is also essential because it factors into the overall value. A chemically pure and structurally perfect diamond is perfectly transparent with no hue, or color.

I love the fact that the chemically pure and structurally perfect diamond is perfectly transparent. The heat, pressure, cutting and polishing that a disciple goes through is to get us to a place where there is no discoloration in us in terms of sin. Total transparency means there is no hidden flaws in us caused by sin, no trace of flesh that cause the light of God not to be reflected in and through us. I truly believe when the sons of God are manifested in the earth, they will walk in the fullness of the glory of God. *"But we all, with open face beholding as in a glass the glory of the Lord, are changed into the same image from glory to glory, even as by the Spirit of the Lord"* *2 Corinthians 3:18(KJV)*. The sons of God will go from justification to sanctification to glorification, which is the ultimate goal of every son. I believe this is the level Paul referred to when he said, *"I press toward the mark for the prize of the high calling of God in Christ Jesus, Philippians 3:14(KJV)*. *"I press"* is the same verb translated as *"I follow after"* in Philippians 3:12, which carries the idea of an intense endeavor. The Greeks used it to describe a hunter eagerly pursuing his prey. Lazy slothful believers will not attain *"the prize of the high calling of God in Christ Jesus."* The chosen few are willing to press and they will inherit that coveted position of the high calling.

The highest calling a person can have is to walk fully in God's glory. To get to that level of glory requires a metamorphosis that can only be experienced when the Holy Spirit and the word of God work together in our lives to conform us to the image of the Lord Jesus. For this level of glory to be attained, the Word has to be a cutting tool in our lives to cut away the dross of the flesh so the oil of the Holy Spirit can illuminate our lives. Paul told the Corinthians, *"Know ye not that they which run in a race run all, but one receiveth the prize? So run, that ye may obtain. And every man that striveth for the mastery is temperate in all things. Now they do it to obtain a corruptible crown; but we an incorruptible"* *1 Corinthians 9:24-25(KJV)*. I believe *"one"* as the apostle used it, speaks of a remnant; a company of over comers who have endured the purification process.

There is nothing temperate about the carnal man, on the contrary his sole purpose and desire is ungodliness. Paul used the Greek word *egkrateuomai* (pronounced *eng-krat-yoo-om-ahee*) for temperate; it means to exercise *self-restraint*. It comes from the root *egkrates* (*eng-krat-ace*); which means, *to be strong or masterful in something, to exercise self-control*. The carnal nature of a person desires everything but temperance and self-control and for this reason God has to use His word as a cutting tool to cut away the root of carnality that was in us from the day we were born.

His word not only cuts but polishes and completes a process in us which gives us the totality of the 4C's.

The Disciples 4C's

Consecrated is when the disciple is set apart for the Master's use. God takes him through a cleansing process of cutting and polishing in preparation to use him for His glory. If the disciple is to bring God glory then he has to allow God to consecrate him then sanctify him. When the disciple yields to the process God fills him with His Spirit, giving him a certain level of boldness and confidence needed to accomplish the word he has been set apart to fulfill.

Christ like character is formed in a true disciple that has been filled with God's Holy Spirit through the consecration and sanctification process. He will not settle for anything less than being conformed to the image and likeness of his Lord Jesus Christ. Like a high quality diamond that has a brilliant or ideal cut, he desires to get to a place where there is maximum light reflection in him. He just does not want to shine but he wants to radiate the glory of his Lord.

Consistency is when the disciple exhibits a greater level of consistency in terms of His walk with the Lord. He will not be slothful but zealous for the things of God. He will meditate on the word day and night in order to have a firm foundation. With that foundation He will not be tossed and turned with every slight wind of doctrine.

Complete is when the disciple mirrors his heavenly Father with the sentiments of Jesus last words when He hung on the cross, "it is finished." His vicarious and atoning death had paid the penalty for Adam's sin so the work of restoration God began when Jesus came into the world could be completed. Through the death burial and resurrection of our Lord Savior, and soon coming King, disciples are in a position to have lives that are complete in Him. Complete means nothing lacking and nothing broken, but a place where we live in total balance and harmony with God and His creation. To get to the place of completion we have to be positioned for cutting and polishing.

The Diamond Cutting Process:

Planning: is analyzing the diamond rough from an economic perspective, with two objectives of how a faceted diamond will be cut. The first objective is that of maximum return on investment for the piece of diamond rough. The second is how quickly the finished diamond can be sold. Scanning devices are used to get a 3-dimensional computer model of the rough stone. Also, inclusions are photographed and placed on the 3D model, which is then used to find an optimal way to make the Cut.

Cleaving or Sawing: is the separation of a piece of diamond rough into separate pieces, to be finished as separate gems. Sawing is the use of a diamond saw or laser to cut the diamond rough into separate pieces. God uses the cleaving and sawing process to separate us from people, places and things that will hinder the preparation process. Soul ties and sentimental attachments have to be broken because it is difficult for us to leave the familiar to embrace His promise.

Bruting: is the process whereby two diamonds are set onto spinning axles turning in opposite directions, which are then set to grind against each other to shape each diamond into a round shape. Diamond dust is pounded in a mortar to make a diamond cutting blade and the powder then is used for the wheels on which diamonds are ground. *"Iron sharpeneth iron; so a man sharpeneth the countenance of his friend" Proverbs 27:17(KJV).* Our walk with Christ appears to be a grinding one at times, but God allows it because all the rough edges have to be removed.

Polishing and Final Inspection: is done on wheels making about two thousand revolutions in a minute; olive oil and diamond dust is used in the polishing process. The Holy Ghost is the olive oil used to give the diamond disciple the best polish possible. The diamond dust represents the word because the Holy Spirit and the Word of God works together in the cutting and polishing process.

The final stage involves thoroughly cleaning the diamond in acids, and examining the diamond to see whether it meets quality standards. The process to get a beautiful sparkling diamond does not occur overnight. Sometimes months, and even years, are required for the perfecting of a single stone. Once a believer is saved and mined like a rough diamond, he is set apart through a process of consecration, but the sanctification process takes a lifetime. The final inspection of the disciple will take place when the disciple stands before the judgment seat of Christ. At that time every disciples work will be tried by fire to determine its sort.

God expects to get a maximum return on His investment of Jesus in our lives. *Matthew 25* describes three individuals who received talents from their Lord to invest. The one who received one talent hid it and was rebuked by the Lord and the talent was taken from Him. God did not send Jesus to give His life a ransom for us, to bring us through the fire, and to cut and polish us so we can sit in church, look pretty and keep the pews warm. The return on His investment that He is looking for is we must advance His kingdom by winning souls and making disciples. Our experience in the fire and pressure and the cutting and polishing process was to give us the look and the toughness to deal with any opposition we face when bringing bound individuals out of darkness into His marvelous light.

It is hard to conceive of a time when a disciple gets to the place where he is totally delivered from every carnal thought, word and deed, but what is impossible with man is possible with God. Enoch is described in the book of Jude as the seventh from Adam. Seven is God's number of perfection and completion. I believe Enoch had reached a place in his walk with God where he attained a level of perfection in terms of his maturity in God. I am not going to go as far as saying he reached a state of sinless perfection because the Bible does not say that. The Bible does says he was translated because he pleased God *"By faith Enoch was translated that he should not see death; and was not found, because God had translated him: for before his translation he had this testimony, that he pleased God"* Hebrews 11:5(KJV).

When Gideon went to battle against the Midianites the instruments used for victory were an empty vessel, a lamp, a trumpet, and a sword. His army of three hundred was divided into three companies. He placed a trumpet in every man's hand with lamps in the pitchers. Before their attack on the enemy the men were instructed to blow the trumpet and break the pitchers. When the trumpets were blown, the pitchers broken and the lamps held in their hand, they cried, *"The sword of the Lord, and of Gideon"* Judges 7:20(KJV). Their enemies fled when they executed the battle plan. The revelation here is the disciple is God's chosen vessel, the lamp is the light of the Holy Ghost, the sword is the word of God in our mouths, and the trumpet is the word of praise that gives Him glory and routs our enemies. The light cannot shine unless the vessel is broken. Our lights cannot shine unless our vessels are broken or cut to God's specification.

Jesus was cut by God the Father on the cross for our sins so the complete light of God could shine in our hearts. Jesus is just like the Father in that there is no "variableness neither shadow of turning in Him." Whatever way you look at Jesus, all you will see is light. Pilot, the Roman governor, had Jesus examined and found no fault in him, which simply means He had no sin. *"And Pilate, when he had called together the chief priests and the rulers and the people, Said unto them, Ye have brought this man unto me, as one that perverteth the people: and, behold, I, having examined him before you, have found no fault in this man touching those things whereof ye accuse him"* Luke 23:13-14(KJV).

The Greek word for examined is anakrino (pronounced: an-ak-ree'-no); it means, *to scrutinize, to investigate,* or *to interrogate.* As foresaid, the best shape and proportion of a diamond comes through knowledge, which allows the diamond cutter to work out the path of any ray of light passing through it. The path Jesus took to be able to be the ultimate reflection of God's light is the path of the cross. The vessels He has chosen to carry His light will be taken through a pathway which requires them to be subjected to intense heat and pressure. *"But he knoweth the way that I take: when he hath tried me, I shall come forth as gold" Job 23:23(KJV).*

The Hebrew word tried there is *bachan* (pronounced *baw-khan*) and it means *to test (especially metals); to examine, to prove* or *to try.* Like a precious piece of gold, Job was subjected to the heat and pressure of the furnace until all impurities were removed. The amazing thing is the Bible describes him as perfect and upright. God told Satan there was no man in all the earth like Job. Wow, what an endorsement by God. However, on the contrary, this shows that no matter how saved you think you are – no one has "arrived". If God found Job to be perfect but still felt the need to subject him to fire, why should we be exempt from test and trials? His perfection and his uprightness were proven to Satan through the fire. When the children of Israel were traveling through the wilderness to get to the promised land, Moses spoke these words to them, *"An thou shalt remember all the way which the LORD thy God led thee these forty years in the wilderness, to humble thee, and to prove thee, to know what was in thine heart, whether thou wouldest keep his commandments, or no" Deuteronomy 8:2(KJV).*

The children of Israel were diamonds pulled out of the rough; they were literally pulled out of slavery in Egypt by God. They were chosen to bring forth the Messiah who would be the light to the Gentiles. They needed to be cut and polished so the light of God could come forth to the nations. The forty year wilderness sojourn was God's instrument, His cutting and polishing tool to remove the thought patterns picked up in Egypt. Forty is the number in scripture which represent testing, trial, and probation. The pathway God led them through in the wilderness was His angle to cut away the things which dulled the light. He had to cut away things that hindered them from being humble before Him. He had to prove them in the heat and pressure of their wilderness experience to determine if they would keep His commandments. The Hebrew word for *"prove"* is *nacah* (pronounced *naw-saw*); it means *to test, to try or to tempt.* God already knew what was in their hearts and that is why they went into the wilderness; He was proving to them what was in their hearts.

Jesus had His own wilderness experience after His epiphany at the Jordan River and after His baptism by John. After the Dove representing the Holy Spirit descended on Him and the Father's voice spoke from heaven, the Spirit led Him into the wilderness to be tempted by the Devil *Matthew 3:16-17, 4:1-2(KJV)*. The Greek word for *"tempted"* is *peirazo,* (pronounced pi-rad-zo); it means to *test, to scrutinize, or to discipline.* Jesus spent forty days and forty nights in the wilderness being tested by the adversary; the testing was so grueling angels had to minister to Him when it ended. He was able to pass the test and the scrutiny by standing on the word of God. He came out of the wilderness and began His public ministry with power and authority. Like the children of Israel, Jesus, Job and others chosen by God in the scriptures to be His gold and His diamond in the earth, our vessels will have to be tested and scrutinized to determine if there is any trash or impurities that will block the light. We know Jesus was pure as He declared, *"for the prince of this world cometh, and hath nothing in me" John 14:30(KJV)*.

LIKE A DIAMOND, GOLD IS A PRECIOUS COMMODITY. PURE GOLD HAD TO WITHSTAND EXTREME TEMPERATURES TO REMOVE IMPURITIES. CARBON ATOMS ENDURE EXTREME HEAT AND PRESSURE TO BECOME A ROCK FORMING DIAMOND, AND THEN THE GEMOLOGIST USES PRECISIONS CUTS TO FACILITATE THE BEST PATHWAY FOR LIGHT.

Chapter 3
A Diamond's Light

*Every diamond is a pathway to light; when it's
a real diamond there are no words*

The entrance of God's word gives light and understanding to the simple. According to the creation account in the book of Genesis, when God created the heaven and the earth, the earth was without form and void and darkness was upon the face of the deep. *"And God said, Let there be light: and there was light" Genesis 1:3(KJV).* The word Genesis means beginnings so we see from the very beginning the LORD God Almighty is the source of the creation and the giver of light. The void and dark earth described in Genesis is similar to the life of a person who does not know the Lord Jesus in the pardoning of their sins. An individual in such a void and darkened state can have the look and sound of someone moral, but God knows the condition of every heart that has not surrendered to His Son Jesus Christ. He sees beyond the public image and the various masks we wear during the course of our lives. In his play, *As You Like It*, William Shakespeare opens with this monologue spoken by the melancholy Jaques in Act II Scene VII: *"All the world's a stage, And all the men and women merely players: They have their exits and their entrances; And one man in his time plays many parts."*

Once an individual comes to faith in Jesus he has to be prepared to have all worldly and pseudo religious masks removed. In the world, masks are worn to hide or cover the results of dark deeds done in the flesh. A person might be a priest and have a veneer of piety but struggle with pornography or other forms of perversion; he may use a religious mask to cover the darkness that consumes his mind, causing him to act out his perverse thoughts. Another individual may wear a mask of being happily married but after dark is curb crawling to solicit prostitutes. The list is endless and we all have masks that we wear or have worn at some point in our lives to impress or make others believe we are something we are not. God sent Jesus into the world to dispel the darkness so we can be set free from the bondage and live a life that is transparent before Him. There isn't anything done in the dark that will not be revealed in the light so the onus is on each individual to bring his or her deeds into the light so they can be approved by God. People may be able to deceive friends, family, co-workers, and church members for a while but nothing is hidden from our omnipotent, omniscient, omnipresent and sovereign Father.

His omniscient eyes are able to gaze deep within the heart and soul of every person. Man can only see the face but God sees and knows the heart. God not only sees the heart, He knows exactly what lies therein. People often repeat the saying, "God knows my heart" but this should not be a comfort, because the Bible declares, *"The heart is deceitful above all things, and desperately wicked: who can know it" Jeremiah 17:9(KJV)?* The Hebrew word for heart is *leb* and it speaks of *the feelings, the will* and the *intellect of a person. Bible Doctrines for Today* states, "God created man in his own image, which simply means man is a "shadowed image" of his maker. Like God, man has intellect, emotion or feeling and will. Man can think, use language, determine his direction and make choices" (Bere, 2011, p.158). Thus, it represents the very center of a human being. At the very least a person without the light of Christ shining in their heart has a nature that is deceitful above all things and desperately wicked.

I thank God for Jesus Christ because by His blood we are cleansed and through the indwelling of the Holy Ghost, God can change the deceitful wicked heart into a heart of love and compassion. God can create a new heart in any person willing to repent and call on Jesus for salvation. It does not matter the nature or the wretchedness of the sinful heart, by yielding the heart to Jesus, transformation and restoration can and will take place. *The psalmist David declared, "Create in me a clean heart, O God; and renew a right spirit within me" Psalm 51:10(KJV).* David is described in the Bible as a man after God's own heart but his prayer of repentance in *Psalm 51* came after committing adultery. On a human beings best day he is capable of the most heinous act. When a seemingly mild mannered citizen is arrested for some grave act, neighbors will say, *"He seemed like such a nice man."* The individual may have worn the mask of a nice man but behind the mask was someone being controlled by an addictive personality. If neighbors could have seen the individual's heart they would have known the true person; this is why discernment is very important. Human beings are capable of good deeds but the word of God says a man's goodness is as filthy rags before God. When goodness comes from a circumcised heart burning bright with the light of Christ, that heart is acceptable and its goodness is acceptable to God.

In his book, *The Character of God: Discovering The God Who Is*, Dr. R.C. Sproul wrote these words concerning God's creative ability, *"God spoke. He commanded light to come into existence. Light began to shine. This is what Saint Augustine called the Divine Imperative. The world was created by the sheer power of God's voice. No artist can speak to his painting and create the Mona Lisa. A sculptor would be called a lunatic for standing in front of a mountain and commanding it to turn into Mount Rushmore. Human beings cannot change the course of nature or bring things into existence by sheer talk. But God can. His voice is almighty."* In her book, *"Clean House, Strong House"*, Kimberly Daniels states, *"Prisoners of war are denied food, space and the benefit of light. Day after day, year after year, they are confined to dark cells where the light of day never appears. When they emerge from dark prison cells, they must go through a gradual transitioning into the light. Jesus came to deliver us from the darkness of sin"* (Daniels, 2003, p. 4). The sin darkened soul finds true life when Jesus Christ the light of the world comes into it.

LIGHT DISPELS DARKNESS IN THE LIFE OF A CHILD OF GOD, GIVING THAT INDIVIDUAL AN OPPORTUNITY TO SHINE LIKE A BRILLIANT CUT DIAMOND.

God set the Sun in the sky to be the greater light and the moon and the stars to be the lesser. Jesus is the Son of righteousness, the express image of God's glory, and we are like the moon in the sense that we are chosen vessels to be His reflection in the earth. The true light of Jesus Christ originates from deep within the hearts of His disciples, not in superficial external forms of religious activity. Committed Christians are not part of a religion; instead they have built a relationship with Jesus Christ. Religion binds and controls but a committed relationship with Jesus sets free. The Sun is the earth's natural source of light, and the Son is the believer's natural and sole source of light. Outside of the Son our lives would be without form and void of Godly direction as the earth was before God commanded the light to shine. In the Biblical account of the return of the Bridegroom, the five foolish virgins are in stark contrast to the five wise because the foolish had no oil in their lamps when the Bridegroom returned.

The foolish virgins allowed their oil to run out and when the Bridegroom came they could not go with Him to the marriage. All the virgins had lamps and they all trimmed their lamps but the foolish did not realize that their lamps were void of oil. This is the reason why introspection and self-analysis is so important. Children of God must constantly do a fruit or light check to make sure there is oil in our lamps. The Bridegroom's return will be sudden and it will not be pleasant to be on the outside knocking in a futile attempt to get in. The Holy Ghost is the Oil and the children of God are the lamps; it is He who gives revelation to our minds for a greater understanding of God our Father and our Lord Jesus Christ. The brilliance found in the Christian vessel is there because the Holy Ghost is allowed to dominate. He prepares God's people for the marriage supper of the Lamb and gets them ready for His return. How did the foolish virgins get to the place where they had no oil when the Bridegroom returned? The answer is they reached a place of reliance on self instead of constantly yielding to the Holy Spirit. There has to be a constant surrendering of our wills to Christ through the Holy Spirit. When Christ walked the earth He stayed in constant communion with His Father and was led by Holy Spirit.

Wherever He went the people saw a great light. At twelve years of age he was able to say to His parents, *"wist ye not that I must be about my Father's business" Luke 2:49(KJV).*

When we have a zeal for the Father's business we will continually be yielded to His Spirit, reflecting and refracting His light. Capturing the reflection and refraction of light in and through a brilliant cut diamond is breath taking. Every gem owes its brilliance, its fire, and its color to light, the play of light, its reflection and its refraction. It is to Jesus Christ the light of the world that every disciple owes their brilliance, their fire, and their light. Outside of Jesus Christ there is no true brilliance, fire, or light. He is the perfect reflection of the glory of God. In His letter to the Colossians the Apostle Paul declared; *"For in Him dwelleth all the fullness of the Godhead bodily" (Colossians 2:9).* Jesus Christ our savior carried all the fullness of the Godhead bodily when He was on the earth; outside of Him no human being can be complete. It does not matter how much education, wealth, and prestige one may have; without Jesus they will always lack the true light and brilliance of God. God created every human with a desire to know Him and have communion with Him through our spirit, which is our God conscious. True darkness is a lack of knowledge of the only wise God and Father of our Lord Jesus Christ.

Philip asked Jesus to show them the Father and it would suffice them, *"Jesus saith unto him, Have I been so long time with you, and yet hast thou not known me, Philip? He that hath seen me hath seen the Father; and how sayest thou then, Shew us the Father" John 14:9(KJV).* Almighty God dwells in unapproachable light so the only way a person can know and see Him is through the eyes of Jesus. Jesus' purpose in the earth was two-fold, to destroy the works of darkness and to reveal the heart of the Father to the sons. Jesus is the perfect gift sent from God. He paid the ultimate price for us by dying on the cross for our sins. He did this so His chosen vessels can retain and reflect His light. Our hearts must be circumcised and purged of everything that will hinder the light. The desires of the carnal nature, when acted upon, will hinder the absorption and reflection of His light because the carnal nature does not want God to get the glory; it seeks its own glory. Our light has to shine like a lamp set on a hill so men can see it and give our Father the glory due to His name. Each vessel chosen by God to shine with the light of Jesus Christ is unique and peculiar like the luster of a brilliant cut diamond. The luster of each diamond is peculiar to that gem, and is called *adamantine*. The luster is like a finger print as it is not found in any other gem. The amount of light a diamond reflects or refracts is dependent on the cut and the polish. The brilliance of a diamond is sometimes termed the fire or the life. The brilliance is determined by the play of light in the stone, upon the path of rays of light in the diamond.

The Cutting Edge

When a diamond is cut in such a way that every ray of light passing into it follows the best path possible for producing pleasing effects upon the eye, the diamond is considered perfectly cut. The master diamond cutter proportions his stone in-order to achieve a perfect cut diamond. The best shape and proportion of a diamond comes through knowledge which allows the diamond cutter to work out the path of any ray of light passing through it. This knowledge is made of the essential part of optics, and the laws which have to be used.

Three fundamental laws: Reflection, Refraction and Dispersion

Are you on the cutting table of God the master diamond cutter at the present time? There is a divine purpose for your process and the purpose is for your life to manifest His laws of reflection, refraction and dispersion. The cutting table is not a pleasant place for our flesh and that is why you can hear the flesh scream with each cut or incision that is made. His word is like a cutting blade made out of diamonds in that it can cut through the tough steel of our flesh in-order to remove pride, arrogance and other things embedded deep within our hearts; these things must be removed so His light can be reflected, refracted and dispersed to a dark world. *"For the word of God is quick, and powerful, and sharper than any two-edged sword, piercing even to the dividing asunder of soul and spirit, and of the joints and marrow, and is a discerner of the thoughts and intents of the heart" Hebrews 4:12 (KJV).*

It is vital to endure the rigors of His cutting table to shine. Surgery is not pleasant but it is necessary to remove things that are infecting the mind, body and soul. He will give you the strength needed to endure the cutting because He loves you and wants to get the best out of you. Do not attempt to go through any form of pruning in your own strength; it is best to just rest in Him and allow Him to complete the process. Once the process is complete you will be a reflection of Him and not self. When your nature is on display people do not see God, hence the need for cutting or polishing. When diamonds are taken from the mine they are translucent, rough and dull, hence the term, *Diamond in the rough.* It is not until a jeweler cuts and polishes them that they will sparkle and shine. This process can raise the value by fifty percent. Fifty is the number for Pentecost and Pentecost represents the outpouring of the Holy Spirit in human vessels. God brings the fire which aids in the cutting and polishing. When He is not indwelling the vessel, the vessel lacks luster and will not have much value.

Reflection

Random House, Webster's Collegiate Dictionary defines the word reflection as, *"The return of light, heat, or sound after striking a surface."* Reflected light in a diamond occurs when a portion or the whole of the light striking the surface is thrown back and does not cross over from one medium to another. The nature of the surface of reflection determines the type of reflection. When the surface is highly polished the reflection is perfect and an image is formed. This is evident in mirrors, polished metals or gems. When the surface is dull the reflected light is then more or less scattered and diffused. In a diamond, the first kind of reflection is important because of its extreme hardness; a diamond takes a very high grade of polish and retains it practically forever.

Refraction

When a light beam passes from a material of lesser optical density (e.g., air) to a material of greater optical density such as the diamond; that light will slow in speed. It will also bend in direction, unless the beam strikes perpendicular to the surface; this bending is called refraction. A beam of light will bend toward the normal when entering a diamond and away from the normal when leaving a diamond. How much of that light's energy is reflected or refracted depends on several factors: the angle at which the light strikes the surface; the optical properties of the material (in this case, the diamond); the wavelength, or color, of the particular ray of light that is striking the surface; and the polarization state (direction of vibration) of that ray.

The refraction of light is the most commonly observed phenomenon, but any type of wave can refract when it interacts with a medium, when sound waves pass from one medium into another or when water waves move into water of a different depth. In optics, refraction occurs when waves travel from a medium with a given refractive index to a medium with another at an angle. At the boundary between the media, the wave's phase velocity is altered, usually causing a change in direction. Its wavelength increases or decreased but its frequency remains constant. Refraction can be seen when looking into a bowl of water. Air has a refractive index of about 1.0003, and water has a refractive index of about 1.33. If a person looks at a straight object, such as a pencil or straw, which is placed at a slant, partially in the water, the object appears to bend at the water's surface. This is due to the bending of light rays as they move from the water to the air.

Once the rays reach the eye, the eye traces them back as straight lines, more commonly termed, lines of sight. The lines of sight interest at a higher position than were the actual rays originated. This causes the pencil to appear higher and the water to appear shallower that it really is. The depth that the water appears to be when viewed from above is known as the apparent depth.

Dispersion

In optics, dispersion is the phenomenon in which the phase velocity of a wave depends on its frequency, or alternatively when group velocity depends on the frequency. The most familiar example of dispersion is probably a rainbow, in which dispersion causes the spatial separation of a white light into components of different wavelengths (different colors). In a prism, material dispersion (a wavelength-dependent refractive index) causes different colors to refract at different angles, splitting white light into a rainbow.

The Light of God's Countenance

"Blessed is the people that know the joyful sound: they shall walk, O Lord, in the light of thy countenance" Psalm 89:15(KJV). The Hebrew word for countenance is *"panah" (pronounced paw-naw')* and it means, *to turn, to face, i.e. appear, look, etc.* There is a remnant, a people who have come through the purifying fire and the furnace of affliction. They are not interested in titles or being seen, not interested in using the gospel for personal gain; their sole interest is seeing the glory of God manifested so lives can be transformed. They want the light of the glorious gospel of Christ to shine in and through them. They do not want men to see self or carnality when they see them; on the contrary, they want their light to shine so men can see their good work and glorify their Father in heaven.

"Arise, shine; for thy light is come, and the glory of the Lord is risen upon thee. For, behold, the darkness shall cover the earth, and gross darkness the people: but the Lord shall arise upon thee, and his glory shall be seen upon thee. And the Gentiles shall come to thy light, and kings to the brightness of thy rising" Isaiah 60:1-3 (KJV). These three verses of   Isaiah chapter 60 speak of a time of unprecedented darkness and debauchery in the earth. I take solace in one thing, in the midst of the darkness and gross darkness, God has a company of saints who will arise and shine because the light of His glory shall be seen upon them.

When Isaiah prophesied about a people arising and shining with the light and the glory of God, he was speaking about a time when Israel would shine with the glory of God and reveal His glory to the nations. I believe the Church of Jesus Christ will be an integral part of that process because the redeemed (according to Paul), that make up His church have been engrafted into the promise like a wild olive branch.

Only God knows exactly how His plan to manifest His glorious light through His people will unfold, but I do know that God will not leave the true Church of the Lord Jesus out of that equation; after all, the redeemed will not be taken through a process of heat, pressure, cutting and polishing only to hide them when gross darkness covers the people. Chosen Israel and redeemed gentiles who have been brought out of darkness into His marvelous light will arise and shine in what Sid Roth calls "one new man." Every child of Christ who has to endure hardship like a good soldier can take comfort in the fact they will be called to shine forth and radiate His glory at the opportune time. Disciples may have to suffer for a season at the present time but at the opportune time we will arise from the place of suffering beaming with the light of His glory. Suffering is not easy but we can take comfort during times of suffering when we understand that suffering is tied to glory. The Apostle Peter summed it up beautifully when he declared, *"The elders which are among you I exhort, who am also an elder, and a witness of the sufferings of Christ, and also a partaker of the glory that shall be revealed" 1 Peter 5:1(KJV).*

PART TWO

Chapter 4
The Mantle

Having the blessings of God on your life and not walking in it
is as bad as being a diamond priced as a cubic zirconium

$\mathcal{D}$ iamonds are formed beneath the surface of the earth, in the rocky portion between the crust and the core known as the mantle. Once God takes us through the compression chamber of heat and pressure to form Christ the solid Rock in us; we arrive at a dimension where we can carry His mantle. Walking with Christ is not for the faint of heart because of the intense warfare His disciples must endure. People satisfied with mere religion will not have to endure the testing and trials disciples must endure to carry the mantle of Christ.

Elisha's prophetic ministry began when he received a double portion of Elijah's spirit; upon receiving the double portion, he picked up Elijah's mantle when the prophet was taken up in a chariot of fire. It is no coincidence that Elijah's exit from the earth was through a chariot of fire. He had endured fiery tests and trials while he stood for God against the Baal worship introduced to the nation by King Ahab's wife Jezebel. Elijah knew the God who answered by fire and Elisha served Elijah faithfully until he was caught up to heaven. Some folks want to wear the mantle and receive the double portion but are they willing to be humble and serve true men and women of God faithfully? God signified that Elisha had received the double portion of Elijah's spirit when he took the mantle, smote the waters, and said, *"Where is the LORD God of Elijah 2 Kings 2:14(KJV)?* The waters parted and Elisha was able to cross over, and began to walk in his prophetic ministry.

When the king of Moab rebelled against the king of Israel after the death of Ahab, the king of Israel asked Jehoshaphat the king of

Judah to go with him in battle against the Moabite king. When they arrived at a place that had no water, Jehoshaphat said, *"Is there not here a prophet of the LORD, that we may inquire of the LORD by him? And one of the king of Israel's servants answered and said, Here is Elisha the son of Shaphat, which poured water on the hands of Elisha.* King Jehoshaphat responded by saying, *"The word of the LORD is with him 2 Kings 3:11-12(KJV).* An individual is not a prophet because he assumes the title of prophet. A prophet is not someone who tells us what we want to hear so he can get us to give a good offering. A prophet is someone chosen by God to bring forth His message to the people. Elisha was first identified as the servant who poured water on the hands of Elijah. Both kings knew of the mighty works of God done by Elijah. What a powerful testimony when it can be said of someone, "the word of the LORD is with him." The word of the LORD was with Elisha because he was faithful in His service to Elijah. When we learn to humble ourselves and be faithful in another man's ministry, God will promote us in due season and give us a more sure word of prophecy. Elisha carried a mighty anointing and did twice the miracles of Elijah because of the mantle.

To wear the mantle of the Lord Jesus and advance His kingdom will require a great deal of sacrifice. Like Elisha before us we will have to leave loved ones and precious things if we are to carry His mantle. Jesus set the bar very high when He declared, *"If any man come to me, and hate not his father, and mother, and wife, and children, and brethren, and sisters, yea, and his own life also, he cannot be my disciple. And whosoever doth not bear his cross, and come after me, cannot be my disciple" Luke 14:26-27(KJV).* We must understand the context in which Jesus spoke those words. We know He came to reveal the heart of His Father which is a heart of love so why would He use such a strong word as hate? Jesus was on His way to die on the cross and He needed those around Him to understand the true cost of discipleship. True discipleship will challenge us to sacrifice everything to follow Jesus and wear His mantle. True discipleship is extremely difficult, and that is why many believers have relegated themselves to being mere church members. Jesus was telling His listeners that loyalty to Him must take precedence over loyalty to family and self. He told them they had to carry their cross. The cross will test our willingness to forsake all to follow Jesus.

When a criminal was crucified in the Roman Empire, the person was often forced to carry his cross part of the way to the crucifixion site. Carrying his cross through the heart of the city meant that the Roman Empire was right in imposing the death sentence. Jesus told His disciples that they would be witnesses for Him after they received the power of the Holy Ghost. The Greek word for witnesses is m*artus* and it means a martyr. A martyr is someone who willingly suffers death rather than renounce his or her religion. *When the going gets tough church members get going to another church, but true disciples are at another dimension where they are willing to give their lives for Him.* Disciples do not arrive at that place over night. There is a long arduous process of testing's and trials which teach the disciple that the most important thing in life is that in all things Christ must be glorified.

In pseudo Christianity it is all about the individual and how blessed he or she will be. In that arena you will not hear many messages on dying to self and dying for the gospel. The *'profits'* and purveyors of that type of feel good message, tickle our flesh with empty promises of material gain, but seldom challenge us to forsake all to follow the Lord Jesus Christ. Prophets like Elisha and Elijah challenged kings to serve the LORD and not foreign gods. They risked their lives to stand for the righteousness of God.

Jesus' followers in the early church were willing to endure suffering for the gospel's sake. Jesus told Ananias that He would show Paul how much he would have to suffer for His name. Jesus did not promise the believer a rose garden; He said "in the world we will have tribulation" but we should be of good cheer because He has overcome the world. Disciples who are battled tested and ready to carry His mantle, do not run from their test, they embrace it because they know what it will produce. The Hebrew word for *mantle* is *addereth*, and it means *something ample, glory*, or a *robe*. It comes from two root words; the word *adar* and *eder; eder* means *splendor* and *adar* means to *expand*, to be *great, glorious* or *honor-*

able. The mantle of the Lord Jesus Christ is one of honor, glory and splendor. A mantle of glory and honor will be worn by those who have allowed His fire to burn through their crust and their core. Everything in them that is not like Jesus must be totally consumed by the fire.

Pseudo religion has a mantle made of glitz and glamour but no yoke destroying anointing. The mantle carriers will be called the Sons of God; they will have His Spirit on the inside. His Spirit will not dwell in any vessel polluted by carnality, hence the need for his purifying fire to permeate every fiber of their being. People with a form of religion are not interested in going through the process to wear His mantle; like fake diamonds, they have not gone through the same process true believers have to endure. Therefore, just as fake diamonds are in abundance so are religious minded people. True disciples, like high quality diamonds, are rare. Quality diamonds are expensive and precious because the atoms of carbon which produced them were exposed to temperatures in excess of 2200 degrees Fahrenheit and 50 kilo-bars of pressure. The extreme heat and pressure compressed the atoms of carbon causing them to crystallize and form layers which produce a diamond. These conditions occur in limited zones of Earth's mantle approximately 90 miles beneath the surface. The diamonds are brought to the earth's surface during deep-source volcanic eruptions; these eruptions tear out pieces of the mantle and carry them rapidly to the surface. This type of volcanic eruption is extremely rare.

Deep down on the inside of the disciple, God is applying heat and pressure to destroy carnality so a beautiful diamond can be formed. God's purpose and plan for the formation of the diamond is not solely for beauty; He brings a diamond out of the heat and the pressure to be His chain cutting tool. Once He cuts the chain of sin which holds people bound, He can shine His light through them in dark places. He gets glory and honor when our lights are shining and people who sit in darkness are impacted. Jesus said, *"Let your light so shine before men, that they may see your good works, and glorify your Father which is in heaven" John 5:16 (KJV)*. The light cannot shine if the vessels are polluted with pride, bitterness, and perversion. Men will not glorify our heavenly Father when they see or smell flesh. We cannot dress up and put cologne and perfume over mess. God's purifying fire is not for the faint of heart; it is not a place for religious people satisfied with a superficial experience but no depth of root. Disciples who carry His mantle have allowed Him to go deep within their hearts and minds with the flame thrower and the compression tool to burn away the dross that keeps the light from shining. They go through a process that allows the nature of Christ to be formed in them. Like the real diamond, the disciple of Jesus Christ will come to the surface through eruptions. In the case of the diamond it is the volcanic eruptions, in the life of the disciple, trials and tribulations force us out of our comfort zones into places where chains need to be cut.

Disciples who have come through the process of heat and pressure through the mantle are able to discern the authentic from the counterfeit. Satan cannot create but he works hard to counterfeit. During my times of ministering I tell believers, *"If you don't have discernment then you better get caller ID."* Without true spiritual discernment the believer will not be able to recognize a bona fide move of God from the counterfeit of Satan. The Apostle Paul declared, *"And no marvel; for Satan himself is transformed into an angel of light"* *2 Corinthians 11:14 (KJV).* The Greek word for transformed there is *metaschematizo* (pronounced met-askh-ay-mat-id'-zo); one of the definitions is, *to disguise.* When we juxtaposition transformed as it relates to Satan and transformed as Paul uses it in *Romans 12:2* to describe the process the believer's mind has to go through, we see a distinct difference. In *Romans 12:2,* Paul used a word I mentioned earlier, it is the word *metamorphoo* which means to change or transfigure.

Like the atoms of carbon that go through the heat and pressure in the earth's mantle; Disciples who carry the mantle of Jesus go through heat and pressure in order to be changed or transformed into Jesus' likeness. Satan and his ministers disguise themselves as angels of light in an attempt to deceive the elect. Theirs is not a change or transformation but a charade or a masquerade. Jesus declared, *"For there shall arise false Christs, and false prophets, and shall shew great signs and wonders; insomuch that, if it were possible, they shall deceive the very elect Matthew 24:24(KJV).* The elect cannot be fooled because they are able to stand in the midst of fiery trails; once they reach a place of maturity in Christ, they are able to discern things through His eyes and not the eyes of religion. Jesus said great signs and wonders shall be performed by the false prophets and false Christs. The life of Job gives us a good illustration how Satan will attack a servant of God in an attempt to overwhelm him and make him think it is God who is punishing him.

False Mantle

In the second wave of attack against Job's children and his livestock a messenger reported to him, *"The fire of God is fallen from heaven, and hath burned up the sheep, and the servants, and consumed them; and I only am escaped alone to tell thee Job 1:16(KJV).* The fire of God destroys the wicked and their possessions not the righteous. Satan unleashes destructive lying signs and wonders against the elect, but they are not fooled because they know their God. The elect have withstood previous attacks from the enemy and that is why they are not easily moved when they receive negative news. The elect has to know the source of the message being brought; is it a message concerning a genuine move of God, or is the messenger bringing a word from a place of deception? The messenger may be speaking from a misguided perspective and not out of malice, but Godly discernment still has to apply because in times of adversity we must know the true voice of a messenger of God.

The untrained eye of a layperson will not be able to tell a genuine diamond from a fake one. It would be foolish for someone to spend a great deal of money without checking to make sure the diamond they are purchasing is authentic. Gemologists are trained to know the characteristics of an authentic diamond verses a cubic zirconia or a moissanite. A cubic zirconia is a synthetic gemstone, used in jewelry as an artificial diamond. Cubic zirconia became more popular since its appearance is very close to a diamond as cut gems. Cubic zirconia is made from a mixture of high purity zirconium oxide powders stabilized with magnesium and calcium.

The amount of each ingredient is carefully controlled, with certain additives sometimes being used to achieve a similar appearance to genuine diamonds. In other words, a cubic zirconia has to have things added to carry the appearance of a diamond, but a real diamond must have things taken away to become a real diamond.

To the naked, untrained eye the cubic zirconia may have the look of a diamond but upon closer inspection their flaws are revealed. Diamonds receive their purity from the extreme heat and pressure the carbon atoms endure in the earth's mantle. When a good diamond is inspected all you see is layers and layers of beautiful light, not a cornucopia of mixture and additives. When the life of a genuine disciple of Christ is examined, layers upon layers of His marvelous light can be seen. False disciples of the world's religions have a pseudo light that have deceived many. On the surface they may look and sound like the real deal, but on closer inspection you can see and hear the mixture and the additives. They are like cubic zirconias; not fashioned in the mantle through extreme heat and pressure. They come into being through a circumvented process in a man-made or satanic made environment. Unlike the genuine diamond and the fire tested disciple, they are unable to cut steel. People settle for cubic zirconias when they cannot afford to pay the price for a genuine diamond. They want the look of a diamond without the sacrifice of paying the price for the diamond.

Salvation is free but the anointing of God will cost us everything. When Satan moved David to number Israel causing a plague to come upon on the people; the angel of the LORD instructed the prophet Gad to tell David to set up an altar unto the LORD in the threshing floor of Ornan the Jebusite. Ornan offered to give David the threshing floor, the oxen for burnt offerings, the threshing instruments for wood, and the wheat for the meat offering. Some believers would have been happy to get something for nothing because they have the disease of free and the disease of me; they want to get all they can and can all they get. David responded to Ornan by saying, *"nay; but I will verily buy it for the full price: for I will not take that which is thine for the LORD, nor offer burnt offerings without cost"* 1 Chronicles21:24 (KJV). David was willing to pay the full price for the land; It was on that site that Solomon built the temple; many believe it was on that site that Abraham was willing to sacrifice his son Isaac; Centuries later, Jesus would teach there.

The True Posture for the Mantle

Joseph with his kinsmen and Egyptian followers halted for seven days at the threshing floor of Atad to lament the death of Jacob. Uzzah died near the threshing floor of Nacon for touching the ark. Ruth reveals herself to Boaz on his threshing floor. The process of threshing was performed generally by spreading the sheaves on the threshing floor and causing oxen and cattle to tread repeatedly over them. When the grain was threshed, it was winnowed by being thrown up against the wind. Chaff is very light and is carried away by even the slightest wind, while the good grain falls back to the earth. The refuse of straw and chaff were burned. Freed from impurities, the grain was then laid up in granaries till used. In Psalm 1:4 the ungodly are compared to *"chaff which the wind driveth away."* In *Ephesians chapter 4:14*, Paul describes the impact the ministry gifts would have, *"That we henceforth be no more children, tossed to and fro, and carried about with every wind of doctrine, by the sleight of men, and cunning craftiness, whereby they lie in wait to deceive."*

Disciples who have come through the furnace of affliction and the process of the threshing floor will be able to stand when the winds of adversity begin to blow. They will be able to spot the purveyors of false doctrine because their carnal minds were melted in the furnace so they could attain the mind of Christ. The fire of the furnace and the pressure of the threshing floor extricate the fleshly tough exterior from the disciple so his ears become calibrated to the sound of heaven. John was on an island called *Patmos* which means *"my killing".* He was able to hear a voice telling him to come up higher. A plane will not take off from the runway with excess baggage that will jeopardize the flight. A believer with excess baggage will not be able to climb to higher spiritual heights or reach the third dimension of God's glory. Synthetic stones are always heavier in carat weight than genuine diamonds, as the material they are made of is denser. Religious people who have not gone through the fire and pressure of purification may look and sound like they have spiritual weight to them, but do not be fooled because everything that glitters is not gold, and everything that is glassy and beautiful is not a diamond. There are synthetic diamonds that are crafted in such a manner they really look like the real thing. The enlightened eyes of the gemologist can tell they are synthetic; the enlightened eyes of the believer will be able to spot a synthetic spirit trying to pass itself off as a true messenger of light.

Chapter 5
Volcanic Eruptions

God has placed treasures on the inside of us, but
we don't boil over until we get hot!

A volcano is an opening, or rupture, in a planet's surface or crust, which allows hot magma, volcanic ash and gasses to escape from below the surface. A volcano erupts when the pressure within the molten magma below the surface becomes stronger than the strength of the rocks on the surface that make up the volcano. Research on _Smithsonian.com_ suggests that the diamonds we see at the surface of the earth were brought there by a very deep-seated volcanic eruption. This eruption occurred a long time in the Earth's history. It was a special kind of eruption thought to be quite violent. We haven't seen such eruptions in recent times; which leads me to believe that this occurrence was probably at a time when the earth was much hotter and the eruptions were more deeply rooted. However, these eruptions carried the already formed diamonds from the upper mantle to the surface of the Earth. When the eruption reached the surface, it built up a mound of volcanic material that eventually cooled, with the diamonds contained within. John chapter ten records how Jesus sent His disciples out to preach the kingdom, to heal the sick, cleanse lepers, raise the dead and cast out devils; He went on to tell them of the opposition they would face as they advanced the kingdom. He declared, _"And from the days of John the Baptist until now the kingdom of heaven suffereth violence, and the violent take it by force" John 11:12(KJV)._

THE VIOLENCE THE KINGDOM SUFFERS IS SIMILAR TO THE DEEP SEATED VIOLENT VOLCANIC ERUPTIONS THAT BRINGS THE ROUGH DIAMOND TO THE SURFACE.

It has been said, *"The blood of the martyrs is the seed or life of the church."* It takes death of self and all the desires of the flesh to bring Jesus Christ the solid rock to the surface of a believer's life. The flesh will not willingly surrender itself to the process of death. Many believers are unwilling to raise the white flag of surrender because they do not want to deal with the violent struggle which takes place between spirit and flesh. They are quite satisfied being carnal Christians living dangerously close to the world's system which is governed by the god of this age. In his treatise to the church at Rome Paul shed great light on the struggle within when he declared, *"For I know that in me (that is, in my flesh,) dwelleth no good thing: for to will is present with me; but how to perform that which is good I find not"* Romans 7:18(KJV).

Paul readily admits that in his flesh or his carnal nature there is nothing good. The will to do that which is good was with him but his difficulty was performing the good. When we study his epistles *as a whole,* we know the answer to this dilemma is in our willingness to completely die to self. There has to be a willingness on the part of the disciple of Jesus Christ to surrender all carnal thoughts and actions; no matter how pleasurable to the natural man they may be. If there is a slight opening in us in terms of our desire for something that pleases our flesh, the adversary will exploit it for evil.

When Paul said he could not find out how to perform the good, he wants the reader to have an understanding of the gravity of the battle that exists between the carnal man and the spiritual man. When an individual has not surrendered his life to the Lordship of Jesus Christ the part of him that is dominant is the carnal nature; once he is made alive in Christ the battle begins within him. Paul went on to declare, *"For I delight in the law of God after the inward man: But I see another law in my members, warring against the law of my mind, and bringing me into captivity to the law of sin which is in my members. O wretched man that I am! Who shall deliver me from the body of this death? I thank God through Jesus Christ our Lord. So then with the mind I myself serve the law of God; but with the flesh the law of sin" Romans 7:22-25(KJV).*

There can be a genuine desire in the inward man to fulfill the law of God, but only through the power of the Holy Spirit will an individual have the strength and the fortitude to win the battle that rages within. On our own, we will not be able to resist all the temptations that constantly bombard our minds. Some individuals are tougher mentally than others, but even the person with the strongest will power is no match for the trickery and the wiles of the Devil. He has been at the deceiving game for a long time and if he was crafty enough to cause the fall of Adam who lived in a perfect environment communed with God, then which one of us can stand against Him without the indwelling of the Holy Spirit. The soul of the believer which represents his intellect, will, and his emotions is the battleground for the spiritual warfare that is taking place. This battle is like the violent eruption of a volcano in that it is intense and it is hot. If we yield to Christ in the process the only thing that will die is the flesh. Paul talked about being delivered from the body of death and that statement should be a warning to all believers not to play with the flesh.

No matter how glamorous the things of the flesh may appear we must resist the enticement it offers because the end of it is death. It is extremely difficult to resist the flesh when it craves the sinful things of this world. The power that the Holy Spirit gives us is the might and the authority to resist and gain strength over the flesh when we are surrendered to Him. The battle may be intense but Jesus Christ has won the battle for us. As long as we allow Him to lead us He will make sure we have the victory. I once heard the declaration, *"the hotter the battle the sweeter the victory."* If we try to take matters into our own hands then we will suffer loss and sometimes death, because the ultimate plan of the enemy is to kill, steal and destroy.

Peter was told by Jesus, *"Satan hath desired to have you, that he may sift you as wheat: But I have prayed for thee, that thy faith fail not: and when thou art converted, strengthen thy brethren" Luke 22:31-32(KJV).* Satan has not changed his *modus operandi or how he does things;* the same desire that he had to sift Peter in order to cause faith failure; he has for every disciple of Christ. The disciple must be on guard and know that Jesus is at the right hand of our heavenly Father making intercession for us. Like Peter, we will fail at times, but we must not abandon our faith in Jesus because of failure. When we fail we must arise quickly with a heart of repentance and learn from the failure so we can be strengthened against the next attack.

It takes extreme heat and pressure to turn atoms of carbon into a rock crystal, and it takes volcanic eruptions to get the rock crystal in the form of a diamond to the earth's surface. Therefore, the volcanic eruptions that bring the rock diamond to the surface are parallel to the battles in the life of the disciple that bring Jesus Christ, the solid rock, to the surface of the disciple's life. To further illustrate, let's differentiate between the life of the casual believer and the life of a disciple. The disciple understands that there will be turbulence as the flesh is pulverized so the life of Christ can be seen. The casual believer is satisfied with a mere acknowledgement or belief in Christ but does not have the desire to go through the heat and pressure to have Jesus, the solid rock, formed in him; which in turn means there will be no volcanic eruption.

As for the process of the atoms of carbon forming into a rock through heat and pressure, each carbon atom is bonded to four other carbon atoms. The heat and the pressure cause the bonding, which in turn gives the diamond its strength. In order for the atoms of carbon to bond together, they must be in close proximity to each other. Heat and pressure forms them and the volcanic eruption gets them to the surface. This three step process strengthens every disciple so Christ can be formed and His life can be brought to the surface. If the process is circumvented then there is only a form of Godliness but no strength or power; only a superficial religious experience. The bonding experience through heat and pressure is the only way the crystals can grow into a sturdy diamond. Research shows, that it's the process of atoms locking into place that produces this repeating network. In other words, this structure of carbon atoms eventually grows large enough that it produces crystals that we can see. Each of these crystals, each one-carat diamond, represents billions of carbon atoms that all had to lock into place to form this very orderly crystalline structure.

The Power of Agreement

Unity in the body of Christ is of the utmost importance if the body is to grow into a strong steel cutting diamond. All components of the natural human body have to work in unity for the body to function in the manner in which it was created to function. When one part of the body is not functioning properly, it places stress on other parts. Free, radical or out of control cells in the body can cause cancer and loose extremists in the local church who desire to do their own thing. Anti-oxidants help the natural body to fight free radicals and spiritual anti-oxidants keep the body of Christ unified and strengthened against free radical attacks. In the same manner that the atoms of carbon lock into place to gain strength, disciples must lock into a place of unity to form an unbreakable bond in Christ. We must understand that eruptions will come and they will be violent, but if we stay in a spirit of unity we will be strong in the Lord and the power of His might. Anyone who has ever attended a church that was divided in any form or fashion can readily attest to the fact that such a church is ineffective in carrying out the mandate of Christ.

The Corinthian church was a gifted church, but it was plagued by division. Paul wrote his letter to them and used an example of a natural body to illustrate the importance of staying unified in Christ. *"But now hath God set the members every one of them in the body, as it hath pleased him. And if they were all one member, where were the body? But now are they many members, yet but one body. And the eye cannot say unto the hand, I have no need of thee: nor again the head to the feet, I have no need of you. Nay, much more those members of the body, which seem to be more feeble, are necessary: And those members of the body, which we think to be less honourable, upon these we bestow more abundant honour; and our uncomely parts have more abundant comeliness. For our comely parts have no need: but God hath tempered the body together, having given more abundant honour to that part which lacked: That there should be no schism in the body; but that the members should have the same care one for another" 1 Corinthians 12:18-25(KJV).*

One of Satan's chief weapons against a local church is the seed of discord or division. The disciples of Jesus must bond together when the heat and pressure is applied. There is no place in the body for clicks and schisms. As human beings we understand the challenge we face when any part of our body is sick and not able to function in the manner it was created. Jesus used a strong example to explain how important it is to remove an offensive part from the body. *"And if thy right eye offend thee, pluck it out, and cast it from thee: for it is profitable for thee that one of thy members should perish, and not that thy whole body should be cast into hell. And if thy right hand offend thee, cut it off, and cast it from thee: for it is profitable for thee that one of thy members should perish, and not that thy whole body should be cast into hell" Matt 5:29-30(KJV).*

The ultimate objective of the building of the church by Jesus is to have a unified body that shines and radiates His glory. The ultimate objective of Satan is to fracture and weaken the body through repeated attacks. A weakened body is unable to fight effectively. When a human body is run down through fatigue and a lack of proper nutrition it becomes susceptible to sickness and disease. When the disciple of Christ is not resting in Him and receiving proper nutrition through the word, he is susceptible to various forms of demonic attacks.   The volcanic eruptions do not destroy the diamond because it has gone through the process of intense heat and pressure; the bonding in the heat and pressure gives it the strength and sturdiness to withstand the volcanic eruptions without falling apart.

The Spirit of Homothumadon

Before Jesus ascended to heaven he met with His disciples and told them to tarry at Jerusalem until they were clothed with the power of the Holy Spirit. After watching Jesus ascend to heaven the disciples went to Jerusalem from Mount Olivet and went up to an upper room to wait for the promise of the Holy Spirit. Their posture while waiting was not one of discord and division, but of unity. In Acts, Luke declared, *"These all continued with one accord in prayer and supplication, with the women, and Mary the mother of Jesus, and with his brethren" Acts 1:14(KJV)*. The Greek word for accord there is *Homothumadon* and it means to have the same mind. The disciples had come to a place of oneness and unity in their thought process. When a local church body understands and adopts the spirit of Homothumadon it will experience an outpouring of the sweet Holy Spirit. It was not enough for the disciples to tarry at the same geographical location, but they also had to be at the same place mentally.

Luke used the same word *accord in* Acts Chapter 2 but the meaning is different. *"And when the day of Pentecost was fully come, they were all with one accord in one place" Acts 2:1(KJV)*. The Greek word for *accord* there is *homou* and it means to be at the same place or time, to be together. In other words, you can have a group of people at the same geographical location all at the same time but mentally they are at a different place. Whether it is in a local church, a marriage, or a company; when there is a spirit of Homothumadon the entity will have what the Bible refers to as a *"suddenly"* experience. Let us examine what happened when the disciples were mentally and physically at the same place at the same time.

"And suddenly there came a sound from heaven as of a rushing mighty wind, and it filled all the house where they were sitting" Acts 2:2(KJV). Unity will bring empowerment and it will bring it suddenly. This principle is so strong until it applies even when people unify around an activity that is wrong. For example, when the people came together to build the tower of Babel, they were so unified in their thought and their actions that God took notice. *"And the LORD said, Behold, the people is one, and they have all one language; and this they begin to do: and now nothing will be restrained from them, which they have imagined to do. Go to, let us go down, and there confound their language, that they may not understand*

one another's speech" *Genesis 11:6-7(KJV)*. Unity and the power of agreement brings the power of God down to the earth.

In the case of the disciples, His power was manifested in the filling of the Holy Spirit. Although the people came together to build the tower to heaven, His power came to scatter them. Now let us examine a marriage. A husband and wife can be in the same bed but be miles apart mentally. Married couples must use heat and pressure to help them to bond together in a spirit of unity and not allow themselves to disintegrate or fracture their marriage. The local church must also allow heat and pressure to fuse the entire membership together in a spirit of unity in preparation for the volcanic eruptions that will bring Christ, the solid rock, to the forefront. ***No Unity, No Holy Ghost, No Holy Ghost, No Power!***

It is not a matter of if, but when the eruptions will come to a marriage, a family or a local church. The question is, how will the parties affected respond when the volcano begins to erupt? Will they allow it to cause division or will they allow it to unite them? A house, a local church, or a marriage divided against itself will not stand. When Jesus delivered someone possessed with a devil that caused the individual to be blind and dumb, the Pharisees heard about it and accused Him of casting out devils by Beelzebub the prince of the devils. Jesus knew their thoughts and responded by declaring, *"Every kingdom divided against itself is brought to deso-lation; and every city or house divided against itself shall not stand"* *Matthew 12:25(KJV)*.

Division causes a crack in the foundation and no matter how beautiful the building, the marriage or the church looks, if there is a crack in the foundation, there will be an eventual collapse because at some point an opposition will test the strength of the founda-tion. Some people are surprised when a seemingly good marriage ends in divorce or when a church splits; unfortunately, for those things to happen there must have been a crack in the foundation that was not repaired. People like to keep up appearances and sometimes they will gloss over something that is problematic to make the public think things are well. This type of situation is no different than the human body; a small sore can become infected and lead to amputation at a later date if not treated. Yes, a band aid can be used to cover the sore, but a band aid cannot treat the sore. A strengthened unified body is able to fight an infection with proper treatment. When the enemy tries to infect a marriage or a ministry with division, it is imperative for the parties involved to recognize the culprit and band together in unity to evict him.

The symbolism in the numbers of the atoms of carbon that bond together under the heat and the pressure is fascinating. One atom of carbon bonds with four and four plus one equals five. In the scriptures one speaks of unity, four speaks of the Creator God, His creation, and the creatures therein. The number five speaks of grace. The one true God Yahweh created heaven and earth and redeemed man by grace through faith in the Lord Jesus Christ. If you are currently experiencing a volcanic eruption in your life, I encourage you to allow Christ the solid rock to come to the surface. Remember, diamonds come to the earth's surface through volcanic eruptions. Do not use fleshly, carnal means to attempt to rectify the situation. Instead, yield to the Spirit of God and allow Him to work it for your good, and He will get the glory out of the situation. There is a lot of ash when a volcano erupts but God will give you beauty for ashes. Put on the garment of praise and take off the spirit of heaviness.

The volcanic eruption may be violent and chaotic but there is a purpose for the process. The heat and the pressure previously experienced in the crust and core of your life prepared you for the volcanic eruption that has come to bring Him to the surface. Once He comes to the surface, He will cool things off. In the midst of the pressure of the volcanic eruption, allow Christ to be seen and not the carnal man. It is very easy to respond in the flesh when things all around you are erupting. The flesh does not bring glory to Jesus so we must stay calm in the midst of it all.

In the parable of the sower, Jesus told His disciples, *"The sower soweth the word. And these are they by the way side, where the word is sown; but when they have heard, Satan cometh immediately, and taketh away the word that was sown in their hearts. And these are they likewise which are sown on stony ground; who, when they have heard the word, immediately receive it with gladness; And have no root in themselves, and so endure but for a time: afterward, when affliction or persecution ariseth for the word's sake, immediately they are offended" Mark 4:14-17(KJV).*

Jesus did not say if affliction or persecution ariseth, He said, *"when affliction or persecution ariseth for the word's sake."* The heat and the pressure burned away the chaff so the logos could become a rhema seed in you which took root. The volcanic eruption has come to bring that word forth with demonstration and power. Is it a marital affliction or persecution that is erupting in your life? Use the word of prayer as a diamond cutting tool to cut away the chains that have bound your spouse. Has the eruption come through abandonment by someone you love, church hurt or a deadly diagnosis of an incurable disease? Allow the peace of God which passes all understanding to guard your heart and your mind in Christ Jesus.

The enemy will attempt to bring a spirit of fear through the violent eruption, but remember the words Paul spoke to Timothy, *"For God hath not given us the spirit of fear; but of power, and of love, and of a sound mind" 2 Timothy 1:17(KJV).* The apostle did not say a spirit of fear, but, "the spirit of fear." Fear is a specific spirit sent from Satan to cripple and paralyze a child of God. God sends power and love so His children can have a sound mind. The word power there is dunamis, and it means ability, might and strength. The Greek word for sound as it is used there is *sophronismos* (pronounced so-fron-is-mos); it means *discipline* or *self-control*. Do not use alcohol, illicit drugs or sexual perversion to deaden the pain. Do not panic in the midst of the eruption and lose discipline and self-control; let the love of God rest on you and give you peace of mind. Put the violent, volcanic eruptions of your current trial and tribulation in the proper perspective. There is a word working in your life and that word is causing affliction and persecution to arise in opposition to that word. The enemy does not want the word to come alive in your life and that is why he is attempting to distract you with affliction and persecution. Focus on the fact that the word is working; the evidence that it is working is the manifestation of affliction and persecution.

When God sends a proceeding word to us, it has to be tried in-order to become a reality and not something theoretical or philo-sophical; the greater the level of the revelatory word, the greater the affliction and persecution. The question is, "will you adopt a posture of prayer and praise in the midst of the volcanic eruption or will you wilt under the pressure and the heat? Will you come out clothed in the garment of praise and smelling like the oil of joy, or will you come out with the look and smell of volcanic ash? You may come out of it with a scar like Jesus had when He showed Thomas the nail print in His hands, but the scar is not there to have a nega-tive impact on you, but to show you that God has brought you out and given you the victory.

Paul told the Corinthians, *"And lest I should be exalted above measure through the abundance of the revelations, there was given to me a thorn in the flesh, the messenger of Satan to buffet me, lest I should be exalted above measure. For this thing I besought the Lord thrice, that it might depart from me. And he said unto me, My grace is sufficient for thee: for my strength is made perfect in weakness. Most gladly therefore will I rather glory in my infirmities, that the power of Christ may rest upon me" 2 Corinthians 12: 7-9(KJV).* He operated in an abundance of revelations and there was a danger of his flesh taking the opportunity to exalt itself in pride and arrogance; the same pride and arrogance witnessed in some men and women of God as they stand in pulpits preaching. The messenger of Satan was a high ranking demon sent to buffet him, which means to beat him to a pulp. He sought the Lord for the alleviation of the thorn and God told Him there was enough grace to endure. God's plan was to perfect his strength through his weakness.

Like Paul, we must not complain when we seek the Lord through prayer for the alleviation of the thorn in the flesh, which has erupted in our lives in the form of persecution and affliction. Once we recognize God's grace or His divine enablement and unmerited favor in the situation, we must endeavor to glorify Him. In doing so His power, His might and His strength will rest on us. When we learn to give God glory with the thorn while buffeting is taking place, it sends confusion into the enemy's camp. When he erupts with sickness in our body we have to say like Job, *"All the days of my appointed time will I wait, till my change come" Job 14:14(KJV).* When funds are low and debts are high quote Philippians 4:19, *"But my God shall supply all your need according to his riches in glory by Christ Jesus (KJV)."* There are untold riches in His glory and we have access to it through Christ Jesus.

Wisdom says, take your eyes off the eruption and tap into the glory through prayer and praise. The glory takes you above the eruption, above the affliction and the persecution. The enemy wants us to chicken out and succumb to the spirit of fear but you must soar like an eagle because chickens don't fly but cluck; eagles soar. We have to make a choice how to respond when spiritual volcanoes erupt and manifest in the natural. Are we going to sit down and cry or will we say like David, *"For his anger endureth but a moment; in his favour is life: weeping may endure for a night, but joy cometh in the morning" Psalm 30:5(KJV).* God will turn our mourning into dancing if we adopt the right posture in the time of testing and trials.

There are times when the volcanic eruption we face is brought upon us because of some sin or our refusal to heed the voice of the Holy Spirit. We must not point the finger or blame others but learn from experience so the next time around we can respond with Godly wisdom. The adversary wants us to believe God is punishing us because He is angry but God does not punish His children out of anger; He chastens them because He loves them. He chastens His children so more of Christ can be formed in them. We can have peace in the midst of the storm if we allow Him to lead us through the storm. In the middle of it all, find a way to give God thanks for His will being done in your life. Let the camp of the enemy know that you will not fold from fear because of the level of the violence of the volcanic eruption unleashed against you. God sustained you in the heat and the pressure while Christ was being formed in you so He will also sustain you as Christ the solid rock comes to the surface.

Chapter 6
Genuine Diamond or Cubic Zirconia?

It is wise to carefully examine what comes to the surface;
everything that sparkles is not a diamond

*H*amlet is William Shakespeare's longest play and among the most powerful and influential tragedies in the English language. There is a great line spoken in Act one, Scene 3 of the play by one of the characters named Polonius to his son Laertes, he stated, *"This above all: to thine own self be true, And it must follow, as the night the day, Thou canst not then be false to any man. Farewell, my blessing season this in thee.* Whether it is a counterfeit one hundred dollar bill, a fake gold chain or a cubic zirconia, no one likes a phony. We feel betrayed when we have been duped into believing something to be authentic when it is actually a fake. God wants His disciples to be true to Him and true to themselves, and to others. In a discourse with Jesus, Pontius Pilate questioned Him about truth, "*Pilate therefore said unto him, Art thou a king then? Jesus answered; Thou sayest that I am a king. To this end was I born, and for this cause came I into the world, that I should bear witness unto the truth. Every one that is of the truth heareth my voice. Pilate saith unto him, What is truth? And when he had said this, he went out again unto the Jews, and saith unto them, I find in him no fault at all" John 18:37-38(KJV)*.

Pilate realized after questioning Jesus that there was no deception or fault in Him. He did not seem to realize that the answer to his question *"What is truth"?*, was right in front of Him because Jesus is the truth, the whole truth and nothing but the truth. The untrained eye of a layperson may not be able to discern a genuine diamond from a fake one. I tell people if they do not have discernment then they better get caller ID. There are many spiritual wolves masquerading in sheep's clothing, or better yet cubic zirconia pretending to be genuine diamonds; some counterfeits are so well put together it is difficult to distinguish them from the authentic. We need God's Holy Spirit if we are to discern the vain and the profane from that which is authentically spiritual. Jesus called Him the Spirit of truth; and told His disciples that the world could not receive Him. He told them that they knew Him because He dwelt on the inside of them. There are many references in the scriptures to false prophets and false Christ's who will try to deceive many in the last days. As disciples for Jesus we must be vigilant and watchful to avoid falling prey to a spirit of deception. Jesus declared, *"For there shall arise false christs, and false prophets, and shall shew great signs and wonders; insomuch that, if it were possible, they shall deceive the very elect"* Matthew 24:24(KJV).

Gifts and callings are without repentance so we must be careful not to be mesmerized by the charismatic gifts without having a true spirit of discernment about the person. Holy Spirit gives us the ability to see beyond the façade and the veneer in-order to determine if the individual is flowing in the Spirit of God or another spirit. A story is recorded in 2 Kings where Elisha was passing by a home in Shunem. In the house was a great woman. This woman had spiritual insight and discernment because she declared to her husband, *"Behold now, I perceive that this is an Holy man of God, which passeth by us continually"* 2 Kings 4:9(KJV). The Hebrew word for perceive is *yada,* and it means, *to discern* or *to recognize.* There are segments of the body of Christ that appear to be enamored with prophesy to the point where many people are being fleeced by so called *"profits."* The first thing we must discern when a vessel stands before us to declare the word of the Lord is whether or not the person is walking in holiness. We are not looking for perfection because we are all being perfected.

However, we must look for a heart that is pure before the Lord. God knows the heart of every individual and God the Holy Spirit in us can and will reveal the nature of the individual's heart. The characteristic the great woman of Shunem recognized about Elisha was the fact that he was a Holy man of God. Prophesy must come from a Holy consecrated vessel; not some shyster using trickery, slight of hand or verbosity to finagle money out of unsuspecting non-discerning believers. There is an untold number of women that have been duped into relationships and marriage by men pretending to be someone with character and integrity. These men perpetrated like they were genuine diamonds ready to commit to a monogamous marriage, but as soon as they received what they wanted, the cubic zirconia in them surfaced.

This behavior is not exclusive to men because there are women who use fraudulent means to snare men. These individuals shined like a well cut and polished diamond that is multi-dimensional and multi-faceted when they were in pursuit of the prey; but as soon as they let their guard down and allowed the pursuer access, another personality manifested. Some of them have the spirit of Dr. Jekyll and Mr. Hyde. The former prince charming all of a sudden becomes King Kong. The consequences can be tragic because of the emotional and physical abuse that can leave the victim wounded and scarred for many years. No one wants to spend time and emotional energy in a relationship that will not bear fruit. In the same manner, it would be foolish for someone to spend a great deal of money on a gem thought to be a beautiful diamond without checking to make sure the gem is authentic.

The Master Gemologist

Gemology is the science dealing with natural and artificial gems and gemstones. It is considered a geoscience and a branch of mineralogy. Some jewelers are academically trained gemologists and are qualified to identify and evaluate gems. Gemologists are trained to know the characteristics of an authentic diamond verses a cubic zirconia or a moissanite. *"Rudimentary education in gemology for jewelers and gemologists began in the nineteenth century, but the first qualifications were instigated after the National Association of Goldsmiths of Great Britain (NAG) set up a Gemological Committee for this purpose in 1908. This committee matured into the Gemological Association of Great Britain (also known as Gem-A), now an educational charity and accredited awarding body with its courses taught worldwide. The first US graduate of Gem-A's Diploma Course, in 1929, was Robert Shipley who later established both the Gemological Institute of America and the American Gem Society. There are now several professional schools and associations of gemologists and certification programs around the world"*

Gemstones are categorized based on their crystal structure, specific gravity, refractive index, and other optical properties, such as pleochroism. The physical property of "hardness" is defined by the non-linear Mohs scale of mineral hardness. Gemologists study these factors while valuing or appraising cut and polished gemstones. Gemological microscopic study of the internal structure is used to determine whether a gem is synthetic or natural by revealing natural fluid inclusions, and included partially melted exogenous crystals to demonstrate evidence of heat treatment to enhance the color.

The spectroscopic analysis of cut gemstones also allows a gemologist to understand the atomic structure and identify its origin as it is a major factor in valuing a gemstone. For example, a ruby from Burma will have definite internal and optical activity variance as compared to a Thai ruby." When the gemstones are in a rough state, the gemologist studies the external structure; the host rock and mineral association; and natural and polished color. Initially, the stone is identified by its color, refractive index, optical character, specific gravity, and examination of internal characteristics under magnification. In other words, a man may see a man's face but only God the master gemologist knows the heart of man. There is not a religious mask a person can wear that will fool our Father in heaven. He knows the difference between a cubic zirconia Christian and a genuine diamond Christian.

Cubic Zirconia

Cubic Zirconia is the cubic crystalline form of Zirconium dioxide. It is a synthetic gemstone used in jewelry as an artificial diamond. Because of its low cost, durability, and close visual likeness to diamond, synthetic cubic zirconia has remained the most gemologically and economically important competitor for diamonds since commercial production began in 1976. Cubic zirconia became more popular since its appearance is very close to diamond as cut gems. Cubic zirconia is made from a mixture of high purity zirconium oxide powders stabilized with magnesium and calcium. The amount of each ingredient is carefully controlled, with certain additives sometimes being used to achieve a similar appearance to genuine diamonds. Simulants like cubic zirconia and other laboratory grown gems have an appearance similar to that of a natural gem but have different optical, physical, and chemical properties.

Over the years the use and consumer acceptance of synthetic and man-made gemstones have grown. Over the years people seeking a religious experience have gravitated from the truth of the word of God and settled for an inauthentic religious dogma that allows them to maintain their fleshly appetites. To the naked untrained eye they may have the look of a diamond but they do not have the luster and sturdiness of a real diamond. Diamonds receive their purity from the extreme heat and pressure the carbon atoms endure in the earth's mantle. When a good diamond is inspected all you see is layers and layers of beautiful light, not a cornucopia of mixture and additives.

When the life of a genuine disciple of Christ is examined, layers upon layers of His marvelous light can be seen. False disciples of the world's religions have a pseudo light that has deceived many. On the surface they may look and sound like the real deal, but upon closer inspection you can see and hear the mixture and the additives. These "so-called" disciples are like a cubic zirconia, not fashioned in the mantle through extreme heat and pressure, not brought to the surface by volcanic magma eruptions; neither have they endured the cutting and polishing by the Master Gemologist which gives pure light. Unlike the genuine diamond and the fire tested disciple, they are unable to cut steel.

PEOPLE SETTLE FOR CUBIC ZIRCONIA WHEN THEY CANNOT AFFORD TO PAY THE PRICE FOR A GENUINE DIAMOND. THEY WANT THE LOOK OF A DIAMOND WITHOUT THE SACRIFICE OF PAYING THE PRICE FOR THE DIAMOND. WE HAVE TO PAY A PRICE TO WALK IN THE LIGHT OF THE LORD.

The pseudo light of religiosity will appear to shine for a season but will not be able to be sustained. At some point it will fizzle out like a lit sparkle on the fourth of July. God wants us to shine like a priceless diamond and be tough enough to cut steel. The cubic zirconia can do neither because it has not endured the process of preparation. The purifying fire of God's furnace and the pressure He subjects us to will remove any impurities within us. Once He brings us forth as a steel cutting diamond we will have the ability to withstand the toughest opposition. We will then be able to tell when there is an imitation in the midst. God does not want us to fall victim to the Devil's deception like Eve did in the Garden of Eden. The serpent that enticed Eve was not a hideous looking creature, she probably would not have entertained any conversation with him had he looked hideous.

In *The Basics: A Categorical Bible Study written by Gene Cunning* he gives this explanation on the word serpent found in *Genesis 3:1*, The Hebrew word for serpent is *nachash, which means "the shining one."* Satan the serpent was masquerading as a creature of light then and he is still doing the same today. I tell people that the Devil does not have any new tricks, only new people to trick. Either Eve could not discern the difference between the authentic and the fake or what he offered was so enticing she could not or did not desire to resist it. The truth behind the definition to temptation is it is something you desire deep down within. Sacrifices must be made to obtain the real thing but it is indeed worth it. I was speaking at a local church recently and shared with the congregation the adage *"diamonds are a girl's best friend"*. I told them how a woman's countenance will often light up when she is given a diamond, especially if it is an engagement ring.

The female congregants were very amused when I told them how some women (upon receiving an engagement ring) are ecstatic, but after they see the microscopic look of the diamond in the engagement ring their look become puzzled. God is building authentic Christians to be a part of the wedding feast when the Bridegroom comes. We are not being engaged with a cubic zirconia because our Father in heaven has given us His Son, which is a bright, shining solid rock. Men have tried to connect us to fake gods in the past, but they had no light and no substance. When God saved us through Christ we knew we were given a true, living authentic savior. Our Father's desire is that we live for Him and help others to receive Him so they will not be deceived by so called saviors who are not authentic.

Fake diamonds differ from authentic diamonds in many ways. An ultraviolet light, also known as a black light, will reflect differently in most diamonds; thereby, making it a useful tool in detecting fake diamonds. Once the diamond in question is held under a long wave of ultraviolet light, more often than not, the authentic diamond will reflect a blue florescence. The majority of diamonds on the market will have a blue glow under ultra violet light, but high quality diamonds will not. Cubic Zirconia has a mustard yellow color under ultra violet light and glass will have no glow at all. The true mark of a genuine high quality, diamond disciple of Christ is whether or not he is able to reflect His light. Religious believers are like the majority of diamonds on the market, they have a blue glow but when held under God's ultra violet light they are not high quality. High quality diamond disciples are part of the remnant that have come through much tribulation and attained a greater dimension of light and sturdiness.

They do not have a mustard yellow color but a color of purity that can only be obtained by spending time in His fire. It is no coincidence that the color yellow is sometimes associated with cowards. God will be the ultimate judge of who is the cubic zirconia verses the diamond Christian. Genuine diamond disciples live and speak His word, but a cubic zirconia will attempt to mix His word with a great deal of additives from the world in order to have a religious veneer while satisfying their carnal nature. Satan is the ultimate cubic zirconia because he masquerades as an angel of light, who will use God's word for evil purposes. He tried it during the testing of Jesus in the wilderness; he said to Jesus, *"If thou be the son of God, cast thyself down: for it is written, He shall give his angels charge concerning thee: and in their hands they shall bear thee up, lest at any time thou dash thy foot against a stone"* Matthew 4:6(KJV). He knew and quoted what was written but Jesus was able to discern his corrupt motives and responded by saying, *"It is written again, Thou shalt not tempt the Lord thy God"* Deuteronomy 6:16(KJV).

Disciples must be on guard and be ready to refute messengers of Satan who attempt to use the precious word of God for dubious motives. Jesus told His disciples to, *"let the wheat and the tare grow together"* so we must not be ignorant of the fact that cubic zirconia's will be in the midst of genuine diamond disciples until the time of harvesting.

PART THREE

Chapter 7
Faith Under Fire

Every genuine diamond must be tested

A disciple should always seek to please his Lord. Biblical faith is more than a cursory acknowledgement of the existence of God. When the Bible declares, *"faith is the substance of things hoped for and the evidence of things not seen,"* that simply means having a belief in something that you cannot see. The Greek word for faith is *pistis* and it means assurance, belief or persuasion. The faith that pleases God is the faith that is anchored in Christ with a willingness to obey His word; when that type of faith is active, there must be substance and evidence. It is futile to expect substance and evidence if our faith is not accompanied by a willingness to carry out God's word. It is not the size of the faith that matters; when the apostles asked Jesus to increase their faith, He responded by saying, *"If ye had faith as a grain of mustard seed, ye might say unto this sycamine tree, Be thou plucked up by the root, and be thou planted in the sea; and it should obey you." Luke 17:6 (KJV).* A small amount of faith can get to the root of any matter or situation we face.

I call the faith that activates and demonstrates *"God kind of faith"*. This kind of faith can only be acquired through fiery trials. This is the diamond type of faith that is formed by intense heat and pressure. Every human being was given a measure of faith by God to survive in this world, but that measure has to be placed under fire and heat like the atoms of carbon to become the type that pleases God. The heat and the pressure cause the disciples faith to form layers and layers on top of each other and crystallize into a rock like the diamond.

The *"God kind of faith"* takes the disciple beyond talk to action; it allows him to know God in an intimate way and to trust Him in the heat of the battle. To be promoted from the level of believer to disciple, each one of us will have to endure a process I call, *"faith under fire."* What happens when you or someone you love receive news of a serious medical condition. The news immediately places our faith under fire. Two things happen simultaneously, our faith is placed under the testing of God's fire but it is also tested by the enemy in an attempt to replace it with fear; this is especially true when a tumor is found and there is a risk in might be cancerous.

I received a call from my son today. He informed me that he has to go to Alabama to have a CT scan done on one of his eyes. His pastor's wife noticed that his eye looked funny and encouraged him to have it checked. The eye doctor had an MRI done and a mass was found so he referred him to a specialist. Once I received the news from my son I sensed a spirit of anxiety creeping up on me so I had to calm my nerves and remember the words I share with people when I am ministering. I told my son we will only have a testimony when we are tested. I explained to him that we have to go through various tests in life because it is through our testings that we truly get to know Christ. I encouraged him not to worry and definitely not to allow the diagnosis to open up a door of fear in him. He told me he would remain positive and I told him to trust in God.

A parent's worst nightmare occurs when there is a serious situation with a child. There can be a sense of helplessness when a child receives negative news and the parent has to wait. In times like these, the parent must keep their minds on Jesus and not allow the adversary to bombard their thoughts with fear and doubt. This news of my son's situation has come to me two days before Christmas. Instead of doubt and fear I am making a choice to anchor my faith in Christ and respond in prayer and praise. It is not a matter of if but when a fiery trial will come to place our faith under fire. When we hear of other people going through times of testing and trial we agree to pray for them and sometimes we forget. When the situation arrives at our doorstep it becomes personal and gets our immediate attention.

In speaking with fellow Christians about tragic situations that they or their families face, sometimes I get the feeling they are shocked something threatening has happened to them or someone they love. The fact that we are children of God does not exempt us from fiery trials; on the contrary, the title son of God is what brings the fiery trials. When trials come we must trust God and realize that He has allowed it for His glory. I truly believe that in all things Christ must be glorified; I don't believe that means all good things but in all good and bad things. Diamonds are not formed in a cool beautiful place and faith is not perfected when things are going well. Faith is perfected when a serious test comes our way and we learn to hold on to God's unchanging hands throughout the process.

There are individuals whose faith melts under the heat and pressure of the fire causing them to doubt and blame God. It is extremely difficult to understand logically why some tragic events are allowed by God into the lives of His children. Some of the things we will face in this life will not have logical answers so we have to trust God when we are not able to figure out why. My son has flaws like anyone else but I know he loves the Lord. He has to know that his love for the Lord will not exempt him from fiery trials because his faith in Jesus has to be tried by fire to determine what sort it is. I would even dare to say our love and trust of God will at times be the things that bring the fire. Remember, it was God who pointed out Job to Satan and told him about Job's attributes as a mature servant.

When the fiery trials started in Job's life his wife told him to, *"curse God and die."* Evidently she had a faith meltdown and could not reconcile the fact that her rich, God pleasing husband was suffering with boils from his head to his feet. She was not only devastated by the horror of what befell her husband but the fact that all their children had been killed. All of us can speculate how we would react if struck by such dire and deadly circumstances as Job and his family, but until we are faced with a tragic situation we can only speculate. Once the fiery trial begins and our faith is placed under the fire, the fire will determine our level of trust in God. I believe the fiery trials we endure are commensurate to the level of faith we are called to operate in. I don't believe God is going to give us university tests when we only have kindergarten faith.

When it comes to lip service, many believers can speak and quote scriptures like they will be in the hall of faith one day. Tests and fiery trials determine which believers have the *"God kind of faith"* that allows them to stand on God's word when attacks are coming from every side. Have you ever encountered believers who can quote the word from Genesis to Revelation but as soon as a trial comes they act like it is the end of the world? God is taking the remnant through a series of testing to establish a foundation of childlike faith. Childlike faith seems odd for mature disciples, but the word childlike simply means total trust in God. A child will jump off a dresser into the arms of a loving parent because he has full confidence in the parent's ability to catch him. God is that loving parent and He wants His children to have total confidence in Him. He will continue testing us until all doubt and fear are removed. When we ask something of Him it must be done in faith; when we pray, we must pray in faith.

After telling His disciples to ask and it shall be given unto you, knock and it shall be opened unto you, and seek and you shall find. He said every one that asketh receiveth; and he that seeketh findeth; and to him that knocketh it shall be opened. When the scriptures are taken line upon line, precept upon precept, we get an understanding that people who do not ask seek and knock in faith will not get anything from God. Jesus declared, *"Or what man is there of you, whom if his son ask bread, will he give him a stone? Or if he ask a fish, will he give him a serpent? If ye then, being evil, know how to give good gifts unto your children, how much more shall your Father which is in heaven give good things to them that ask him" Matthew 7:9-11(KJV)?* I truly believe the askers, seekers and knockers Jesus referred to are those asking, seeking and knocking with faith that has been under fire. We cannot expect to receive from God when we are double minded. If we truly believe God then we must speak and act like we believe Him.

The Holy Spirit spoke to me recently concerning the fact that disciples can only expect promotion in the areas where they have been tested. There will be no social promotion in God; before He promotes He will test. Two of the areas where His children have been severely tested are in our health and our finances; the testing of those areas has led to other tests in places like marriage, ministry, and other areas. When I minister I tell my audience that they will be promoted if they are able to pass their tests. Passing comes when we are able to stand firm in our faith as we are taking the exam. Are you in the midst of long term incarceration behind prison walls? Can you overcome spirits of depression, oppression, melancholy and suicide and allow your prayer and praise to cause a sudden violent earthquake to shake the prison doors open for you, like it did for Paul and Silas as described in *Acts 16*? The three Hebrew boys kept their faith in the fiery furnace, Daniel continued to pray in the Lion's den and Joseph was able to sustain from the pit to the prison all because each one of these men kept their faith in God. According to *Hebrews 13:8* (KJV), *"Jesus Christ is the same yesterday and today and forever"*. He has no respect of person so if you keep your faith in Him He will also give you victory.

What type of exam are you taking at the present time? Is it medical, financial, or does it have to do with the loss of a spouse, a family member or a home? Are you dealing with a debilitating disease that keeps your body in constant pain? In the midst of the pain can you stand on the word of faith that says, "Healing is the children's bread?" Have you lost your job, has your business failed and your bills are piling up faster than you can pay them? In the midst of the financial storm can you stand on the faith word that says, "My God shall supply all your needs according to His riches in glory by Christ Jesus?" Have you lost someone you love or are you dealing with the loss of a home through foreclosure after doing all you could to hold on to it? As you face the prospect of having to move in with friends or relatives, or moving from a home into an apartment? Can you stand on the word that says, *"And every one that hath forsaken houses, or brethren, or sisters, or father, or mother, or wife, or children, or lands, for my name's sake, shall receive an hundredfold, and shall inherit everlasting life"* Matthew 19:29 (KJV).

What is your posture in the midst of the exam when the proctor is quiet? Is your posture one of pessimism or is it prayer and praise? Reflect back and draw upon the faith test you have taken to secure previous promotions. God has not only changed the circumstance, it is now a great deal hotter because you are in line for a greater dimension of glory. You came through the last test with prayer, praise and by meditating on His word so for this test go on to another realm of prayer, praise and study. For example, in elementary school you learned how to add, but when you got promoted to middle school you had to learn how to add fractions. By the time you got to high school, addition was apart of every mathematical equation. You see God knows life is going to be a formula; so if all you know how to do is add then you won't be able to apply the concepts to the formula to resolve the problem you are facing. Now for all those that don't like this example because you didn't like math, keep in mind our tests are always open book tests so we can go to the Bible for the answers. God is the proctor of your current exam and if He is silent you should not be nervous; He is teaching you how to stand on His word and apply the answers found in the text to the test questions. God has the answer for every test we will face in this life, so let us endeavor to keep our eyes and ears fastened on Him.

We have the Holy Spirit the Guidance or the Wonderful counselor on the inside to direct us to the place in the word where the answer is located. He is also called the comforter because He brings comfort to a troubled soul during times of testing. Concerning Him Jesus said, *"But the Comforter, which is the Holy Ghost, whom the Father will send in my name, he shall teach you all things, and bring all things to your remembrance, whatsoever I have said unto you"* *John 14:26 (KJV)*. The Holy Ghost is able to teach us everything we need to learn as we mature in Jesus Christ. The Holy Ghost is Omniscient, which means all knowing, but He cannot illuminate or give revelation to a word that you have not read. That is why it imperative that we study the word. Paul told Timothy, *"Study to shew thyself approved unto God, a workman that needeth not be ashamed, rightly dividing the word of truth"* *2 Timothy 2:15 (KJV)*. There are seasons in our lives when we spend a great deal of time and energy studying to make ourselves more marketable and there is nothing wrong with that because we live in this world. However, we are not of this world and we have to make sure that we don't gain the secular world mentality through studies and hard work then lose our soul because it is not anchored in Jesus Christ through faith and diligence to His word.

When our faith is under the fire of God's testing, we should not be troubled in our minds; we should not be grasping for answers to the questions bombarding our minds. We should have a word hid in our hearts for every situation we face. Jesus promised that the comforter would teach us all things; so we must stand on that promise and trust Him. Our foundation is in Jesus and we build on that foundation by applying His word, not only in times of calm, but especially in times of trials. Jesus has spoken many things to us through the Bible and we will need His words to help steady our ships in tempestuous seas. Push pause and summon His precious Holy Spirit and begin to thank Him for bringing to your remembrance words previously spoken by Jesus that can calm fears and wipe away tears in the midst of the present crisis. People will offer all kinds of advice but it is very important to trust God and listen to the Holy Spirit because He is the Spirit of wisdom and counsel. We thank God for doctors when they make a diagnosis and tell us the prognosis, but we must hear what God is saying through the Holy Spirit to receive complete healing. The brightest of minds can fail us but Jesus never fails and the Holy Spirit is never wrong. When we hear His voice and follow His advice, things work out the way God intended them to work out.

As I reflect on the situation my son is facing, I am going to continually encourage him to look for the Christ in the crisis and trust Him in the cross that he has to bear. As a young believer in Christ his faith is still being developed and I believe the level of his current test is indicative of the fact that God has a great assignment for him. His current fiery trial has been sent to crystallize and strengthen his faith like a precious diamond and prepare him for the work the Lord has called and predestined for his life.

It is my responsibility to help him through this process with prayer and words of encouragement along the way. I have come through severe test and trials in my own walk with the Lord so I can share those experiences with him and show him how the Lord used them to strengthen my faith when it was under fire. We read so many stories of individuals like Job in the Bible who had their faith placed under the fire of God's furnace. We can learn a great deal from those who passed and from those who failed. When our faith is placed under the fire it is like a wakeup call; our lives are not the same and it becomes painfully obvious that change can happen in a moment's notice.

The challenge is how do we maintain a sense of normalcy in the midst of chaotic situations? The answer is, we rest in Christ and allow Him to work in the situation. Resting in Christ is easier said than done because the enemy will throw fiery darts of doubt, fear, anxiety, and bewilderment to destabilize our minds. God uses fiery trials to strengthen our faith and prepare us for promotion but the Devil uses fiery darts to cripple our faith in an attempt to demote us. We must be convinced that Christ is with us in the crisis, and out of the affliction comes an anointing. The type of faith that moves mountains and the level of anointing that destroys yokes are not attained in Sunday school classrooms or mid-week Bible study.

We are taught the word in those settings but the realness of the word is learned when the word produces a situation that tries our faith. When we stand on the taught word and pass the test, another building block of faith is added. I can honestly say that the times in my life when I have grown the most in my walk with God are times of testing when I had to trust Him. When things are going well we can become complacent, but we will look to God in prayer or through His word when a crisis arrives. I never thought much about serving God when I was in the world dealing drugs and en-joying the pleasures of sin. However, when that season ended and pleasure gave way to the pain and prospect of a lengthy prison sentence, I picked up a small Gideon Bible in my prison cell and started reading it.

I didn't have faith in God and the furnace I was in was a direct result of my own life of sin, but I had enough sense to know that I was powerless to rectify my situation, so I grabbed the word of

God for comfort. My courage was severely tested when I found out there was an attempt to indict me in the mid-west as a member of an organized drug organization. I am not going to lie and tell you that I was calm, cool and collected when I received the news of the impending indictment. Instead, I was petrified and terrified at the prospect of being transferred to a United States prison after my eight year sentence was up. When I was in the world and faced a serious situation, I drowned my sorrows in alcohol and other ungodly things but I had no intention of going back down that road; I refused to drink the rot gut liquor crudely brewed by the inmates, which only made a bad situation worse. The number one rule of holes is this, *"when you find yourself in one, stop digging."*

Sin placed me in the hole of prison and I was not going to make the hole deeper by indulging in more sin. When I met Jesus through the word, I knew that was the key to being pulled out of the hole. My diligent search through the New Testament gave me knowledge of Him. With the knowledge I acquired, I gained strength and confidence that He would see me through the current sentence and the serious case they were trying to bring against me in the United States. The more I focused on Him through the word the more peace I had during the storms of my sentence. He came through for me and I did NOT have to go to prison in the United States. Hallelujah! If He did it for me He can do it for you because God has no respect of person.

Through that experience I learned to trust Him by standing on His promises in the word whenever a situation arrived that was detrimental. I knew that I could not be presumptuous and live an immoral life and expect God to bail me out when I was in trouble. No, I understood that if the word was going to work for me, I had to apply it to my life. I've had times since those experiences when I have messed up but I knew enough to repent and allow Him to restore me through His grace and mercy. Faith in God should not only help us to trust Him in times of trouble, it should also encourage us to live a life of holiness before Him. Our faith comes under fire when a situation arrives that challenges us. We should take the opportunity to examine ourselves to discern if there are open doors in our lives that God is trying to close. When He speaks a word of correction through His word and we do not heed; He will send a fiery trial to get our attention. The point I am trying to make is this, fiery trials should accomplish two things; they should strengthen our faith but they should also get us to the place where we turn away from ungodly thoughts, words and deeds.

When we are in the midst of a trial it is not easy to understand how God is working things out our good so we have to take Him at His word. He takes us deep down into the mantle of His presence and subjects us to heat and pressure because He loves us and is maturing us for the greater things He has for us. *"For whom the Lord loveth he chasteneth, and scourgeth every son whom he receiveth" Hebrews 12:6 (KJV).* The Hebrew word for Chasteneth is *paideuo* (pronounced pahee-dyoo-o); it comes from a root word which means, *to train up a child, to educate or discipline.* Our Father in heaven uses chastening to bring us from infancy to adulthood. Which parent would expect their child to become a mature well-adjusted adult by giving them everything they asked for? The child would not learn to stand on their own feet or work hard for the things they needed. A loving parent withholds certain things from the child, especially if they are not at a place of maturity to handle them.

As soon as kids get to the age where they can have a license to drive they are ready to borrow their parent's car or petition them for their own set of wheels. The parent knows they cannot turn the keys over to the child because the child wants to drive. The child might not be happy when the keys are withheld from them, but the parent knows that an automobile in the hands of an unskilled driver can be a weapon of mass destruction. Our Father prepares us for adulthood through disciplined testing. Once we pass the test He hands us a set of keys and sends us on our assignment. On this journey called life we will face obstacle courses as we drive towards perfection in Him. We must stay in our lanes and allow Him to direct traffic and there will not be any pile-ups.

Fire tested faith allows us to maneuver through every obstacle we face on our course. Our faith is like a fingerprint in that it is unique to us and the tests we face. Every son has a God ordained journey to travel and God tailors each test for that journey. We can encourage one another but no one can take our exam for us. I was watching the news recently and there was a report about students who were arrested for taking SAT exams for other students trying to get into major universities. The pressure to succeed caused these students to try and circumvent the process by cheating. God will not allow us to circumvent the testing process. The Kingdom of God is the ultimate goal of the disciple and it can only be entered through much tribulation. Like the student trying to earn high SAT scores to gain entrance to top rated schools, the disciple's goal is the prize of a higher calling.

A loving parent will take a hit for their child at anytime, but the child will not develop properly if he is not allowed to sit for his own exams. Like the caterpillar that has to struggle to get out of the cocoon, or the atoms of carbon that have to stay under the heat and pressure until they are crystallized into a rock forming diamond; the sons of God will have to endure their tests of fire if they are to become a beautiful butterfly or a high quality diamond. The purpose behind every test is to determine if the individual being tested has what it takes to be promoted. When I was growing up I would hear people say, *"Talk is cheap."* Well, talk is not cheap when we speak the word of God in faith, which ultimately results in a fire test.

Diamond faith is the type of faith that refuses to yield when the furnace is heated to the max. It is firmly anchored in God and knows beyond a shadow of a doubt that He will have the victory at the end of the test. Faith that has gone through heat and pressure will cut through every chain of doubt and fear that comes to keep God's children bound. Every challenge the child of God faces in his or her life has a specific purpose in terms of their walk with God. He is a loving Father and He will not allow our faith to endure fiery trials without a purpose. There is something God has hidden within us that may only be revealed through crisis and difficulty. We may not understand what His purpose is when we are in the midst of the fiery furnace but if we maintain our trust in Him, we will truly understand the words by songwriter *Charles Albert Tindley "We will understand it better by and by."*

For many, the "by and by" may seem forever, so allow me to challenge your heart. During times of extreme pain; push pause and examine those circumstances in your life. As a matter of fact, don't call them circumstances, rename them DIAMOND MOMENTS! As a result of this refining process, write down what you feel in your heart God is trying to reveal to you. Ask God about the diamond characteristics that you are carrying on the inside of you that the world needs to see. *"He trained us first, passed us like silver through refining fires, brought us into hardscrabble country, pushed us to our very limit, road-tested us inside and out, took us to hell and back; finally he brought us to this well-watered place" Psalms 66:10-12 (MSG).*

Chapter 8
No More Chains, No More Rough

*Now that I have passed my test, I am no longer rough
neither do I go back to that rough state again*

" *Stand fast therefore in the liberty wherewith Christ hath made us free, and be not entangled again with the yoke of bondage"* *Galatians 5:1(KJV)*. When Paul wrote those words to the Galatians he was warning them against the people who were trying to take them back into the bondage of legalism. Through Paul's ministry they were birthed into the Spirit of Christ from the slavery of heathenism and were under threat of being led back into bondage. One of the hardest chains to cut is a religious chain because a person bound with a religious chain thinks they are alright because that is a form of godliness. The religious mind is bound and steeped in religious tradition through indoctrination; this form of bondage is extremely difficult to break without God.

In *Psalm 68*, the psalmist spoke about God bringing out those which are bound with chains. The chains are not only indicative of the sin of rebellion that keeps sinners bound, but also any mindset or thought pattern that has a form of godliness but denies the power of God. Jesus Christ is the ultimate Solitary Diamond used by Father God to break the chains of bondage passed to mankind through Adam; these include physical as well as mental chains, they also include chains of sin as well as chains of religion. Mental chains are much more difficult to deal with than physical chains because more often than not they are ingrained in the individual over a long period of time.

I remember hearing the story of a baby elephant chained to a stake which hindered it from being free to roam. The baby elephant became so accustomed to being chained that once the physical chain was removed the elephant would not go beyond a certain point because in its mind it felt like it was still bound by the chain. God desires to deliver us from the elephant mentality and replace it with the mind of Christ. The children of Israel had to go into the wilderness so God could prepare them to enter the Promised Land. In one of the meetings with Pharaoh, Moses was instructed to say to him, *"The LORD God of the Hebrews hath met with us: and now let us go, we beseech thee , three days' journey into the wilderness, that we may sacrifice to the LORD our God" Exodus 3:18(KJV).*

The number three speaks of resurrection and God was about to resurrect them from the bondage of slavery into the land promised to Abraham. The wilderness is not an easy place to be because it is the place of sacrifice, but it is a necessary place if we are to enter and occupy the Promised Land. God's children must learn to give Him the sacrifice of praise in the wilderness; we must learn to worship and celebrate God in the midst of our wilderness experiences. When Moses was first sent to Pharaoh by God, these are the words he spoke to Pharaoh, *"Thus saith the LORD God of Israel, Let my people go, that they may hold a feast unto me in the wilderness" Exodus 5:1(KJV).* I normally associate the word feast with good food, and I could think of many nicer places to have a feast than the wilderness, but a close examination of the Hebrew word for feast is *chagag* (pronounced *khaw-gag*); it means to *move in a circle*, specifically to *march in a sacred procession*, to *observe a festival*; to *be giddy*: to *celebrate* or to *dance*.

In the secular realm going around in a circle is considered counterproductive, but the Israelites were not called into the wilderness by God to waste time by going in circles. I believe it was a test run for Jericho. Remember how the walls of Jericho came down? Joshua was instructed by God to compass or encircle the city by marching around it for six days. God instructed Joshua to have seven priests bear seven trumpets of rams' horns before the ark which represented His presence. On the seventh day they were instructed to compass the city seven times, and the priest were to blow the trumpets. The people were instructed to shout with a great shout when they heard the long blast of the ram's horn. God told them that the wall would fall down flat when they shouted and it did, allowing them to conqueror the city.

The wilderness is a pit stop of celebration and preparation for the blessing of the Promised Land. If you cannot be giddy in celebrating and worshiping God through a shout and through the dance in the wilderness you are not ready to be promoted to the Promised Land. Remember what happened to the generation who murmured in the wilderness instead of shouting and dancing. If you can shout or be giddy and dance in the wilderness, you are ready for your promotion to promise. The shout of the child of God in the midst of a wilderness experience cuts chains and looses bands. The Hebrew word for shout is, *ru-wa,* and it means, *to mar* (especially by breaking); to *split the ears with sound, to destroy or to make a joyful noise.*

When we learn to give God shabach praise, especially in the wilderness, mountains will become a plain and walls will come down. The word *shabach* means, *to address in a loud tone.* Religious folks might look at you crazy when you let out a shabach praise in their midst but they do not know the level of the depth of the wilderness you are experiencing at the present time so do not allow the glare of their religious stare to silence your radical praise. You need those walls to come down in the wilderness so shout onto God with the voice of triumph.

When I was growing up there was a commercial for a laundry detergent with the name shout. Their slogan was, *"if you want to get a tough stain out, shout it out."* That company was on to something, but I would like to revise that slogan by declaring, *"If you want to get a tough chain loosed, shout it out."* There are countless examples of the effects of a Godly shout in the scriptures. For example, when Jeroboam led the children of Israel against Judah, when Judah looked back and saw the battle before and behind: the people cried unto the Lord and the priests sounded the trumpets; then the men of Judah gave a shout: and as the men of Judah shouted, it came to pass, that God smote Jeroboam and all Israel before Abijah and Judah.

In every congregation the men of Judah, must lift up their voices like a trumpet and shout forth the praises of God. When the praises of Judah go up the blessings of God will rain down. One of the saddest things to witness in a congregation are men sitting around non-chalantly during the time of praise and worship. If they could only receive and act upon the revelation that when the men of Judah are willing to shout the praises of the most high God, many in the congregation will be delivered from the enemies that are in front and behind.

It is with a shout that the return of our Lord and King will be heralded. *"For the Lord himself shall descend from heaven with a shout, with the voice of the archangel, and with the trump of God: and the dead in Christ shall rise first" 1 Thessalonians 4:16(KJV).* Jesus is going to return from heaven with such a loud shout that the grave will not be able to hold saints that have died in Him. I affirm and reaffirm that there is power in the shout. How do you think the walls of blindness came down and brought sight to blind Bartimaeus? It is not a co-incidence that Jesus encountered him as He departed from Jericho. Bartimaeus' eyes were shut up by blindness, but Jesus was about to open them because of his shout. When he heard that Jesus of Nazareth was passing by he began to shout out, *"Jesus, thou Son of David, have mercy on me" (Mark 10:47).* When Jesus heard his shout He stood still and commanded Bartimaeus to be brought to Him so his sight could be restored.

There are times in our lives when meditation is appropriate but there are other times when we have to cast off fear and timidity and shout forth the praises of God. The god of this age desires to keep the minds of people blinded by sin and perdition, he wants to keep them shackled and chained to past experiences, so depleted and depressed that they cannot praise God in the midst of their wilderness. Past negative experiences can be like a ball and chain or a millstone around the mind of an individual, and unless they receive deliverance they will go through life without experiencing the fullness of God and the person He created them to be. There are horrific stories of children who have suffered abuse and grown up unable to get past the abuse even though the abuser was taken out of their lives. Unfortunately, they are mentally chained to the abuse and the abuser so they live with the pain of the experience. I heard someone once say, *"memories don't leave like people do they always stay with you."* There are individuals who have suffered emotional verbal and physical abuse in their marriage and long after the marriage is over they are unable to function in a normal relationship. If their minds are not renewed they end up getting into another bad marriage or relationship due to low self-esteem ultimately causing a vicious cycle. Jesus Christ can take a person that was mentally and physically abused and give them a new mind, by cutting away the mental dross and all the negative effects of past relationships. The victim can become the victor if he or she allows the mind renewal process to take place.

Many people are not receiving deliverance because they spend their lives blaming and hating themselves. The victim must allow Jesus Christ to break the chains of mental bondage that fosters physical debilitation then allow Him to use their experiences to bring someone else with the same chains out of bondage. The chains of death and the grave that held Jesus captive was broken and He desires to empower those who have come to Him by faith to be delivered so they can be His tool of deliverance for others. The psalmist declared, *"Thou hast ascended on high, thou hast led captivity captive: thou hast received gifts for men; yea, for the rebellious also, that the LORD God might dwell among them. Blessed be the Lord, who daily loadeth us with benefits, even the God of our salvation. Selah" Psalm 68:18-19(KJV).*

When Jesus rose from the grave he ascended to the throne room to sit at the right hand of God, the Holy Spirit came to indwell His disciples in order to complete the salvation journey of justification, sanctification and the ultimate prize of glorification. Jesus has given gifts to His body the Church in the form of individuals whom He has ordained and appointed to bring the body of believers to a place of perfection and edification for the work of the ministry. The work of ministry is done when a convert is won to the Lord Jesus Christ, and comes to maturity in Him through discipleship; that disciple then goes out and does the same thing.

The Apostle Paul summed it up best when he wrote, *"But unto everyone of us is given grace according to the measure of the gift of Christ. Wherefore he saith, when he ascended up on high, he led captivity captive, and gave gifts unto men. (Now that he ascended, what is it but that he also descended first into the lower parts of the earth? He that descended is the same also that ascended up far above all heavens, that he might fill all things.) And he gave some, some apostles; and some, prophets; and some, evangelists; and some, pastors and teachers; For the perfecting of the saints, for the work of the ministry, for the edifying of the body of Christ: Till we all come in the unity of the faith, and of the knowledge of the Son of God, unto a perfect, man unto the measure of the stature of the fullness of Christ"* Ephesians 4:11-13(KJV). Perfection or fullness in Christ should be the goal of every disciple, but it cannot be achieved unless every chain is broken and the disciple walks in total freedom.

In the song *I'm Free*, the songwriter declared, *"I am free praise the Lord I am free; No longer bound, no more chains holding me. My soul is resting it's such a blessing praise the Lord Hallelujah, I'm free."* There are many types of chains used by Satan to hold his captives in prison. The only way to freedom for the bound sinner is Jesus the Solid Rock; Jesus the Solitary Diamond. Outside of Him there is no hope of freedom. Man made programs can offer temporary relief from addictions but the chain of carnality that each person comes into this world with can only be cut by King Jesus. When the human soul is bound with the chains of lust, perversion, bitterness, unforgiveness, or any other type of sin, there can be no peace or rest. Men employ various forms and methods to soothe their sin sick souls, but none have a lasting desired effect.

Illicit sex, drugs and other things may offer a temporary escape but ultimately, they exacerbate the problem by opening doors for more chains to keep the soul in bondage. The addict is always seeking a more potent hit of drugs or a more potent sexual encounter that is more satisfying than the previous one. The lascivious and licentious appetite is always craving more in hopes of appeasing an urge that entices or forces the individual to perform unspeakable acts. I believe the soul of every individual longs for peace and rest from this sin sick world, but how to find that peace is a mystery to the masses because Satan the deceiver works diligently to keep them bound in ignorance. I do not believe anyone in their right mind desires to be a heroin addict, a crack addict a pedophile, or some other societal outcast.

There is a spirit of bondage operating in the person's life and it keeps him enslaved to the carnal desires. God's desire is to sever the chain and the spirit of bondage and replace it with the spirit of adoption, where the bound can be made free to cry Abba Father. Addiction to any illicit substance or any negative thought patterns will cause enslavement to the object of the addiction. Satan knows the particular sin that each person has an affinity for; he knows how to package it in a way to deceive the individual into thinking that it will bring only pleasure and not pain. There is not one individual on the face of the earth that is able to resist his temptation without Christ. The Apostle Paul declared, *"For all have sinned, and come short of the glory of God" Romans 3:23(KJV)*. Paul's declaration that every person has fallen short of God's glory through sin is a confirmation that each person has some form of sin he battles with. Satan knows what that sin, weakness or chain is and he exploits every available opportunity to keep people trapped.

Satan is a slave master who tries to keep the sinner under lock and key through a campaign of deception, but Jesus is the great emancipator who has come to set the captives free. The book of Revelation declares it, *"And I saw an angel come down from heaven, having the key of the bottomless pit and a great chain in his hand. And he laid hold on the dragon, that old serpent, which is the Devil, and Satan, and bound him a thousand years, And cast him into the bottomless pit, and shut him up, and set a seal upon him, that he should deceive the nations no more, till the thousand years should be fulfilled: and after that he must be loosed a little season" Revelation 20:1(KJV)*.

I hear many believers talking about binding Satan but Revelation lets us know that it is an angel with a great chain that will bind him. Notice that the angel came down to bind him with the great chain which lets us know that he is loosed in the earth wreaking havoc, but his time is short. He knows his time is short so his goal is to kill as many people as he can by enticing them into sin. His ultimate goal is to destroy them in their sin before the chains that have held them bound can be cut. This is the reason why it is imperative that the redeemed allow the Lord to use us to loose the captives through evangelism and discipleship. We cannot afford to sit idly by in our comfortable sanctuaries while Satan unleashes his destruction upon the nations. God has not set us as the solitary or solitaire diamond in the families of the earth for us to sparkle and shine amongst one another in cushy comfortable meeting places. God wants His children to shine but he wants them to shine where it is dark so the blind can receive sight.

His ultimate plan is that His creation reflects His glory. Sin caused us to fall short of the glory but Jesus Christ came to bridge the gap so those who repent can walk in the glory. When we examine the state of the world today, we understand what Paul meant when he said *"the wages of sin is death."* One would think mankind would see the death and destruction sin has caused and then turn to God in repentance; it appears that the opposite is happening in the world. Instead of repenting, men's deeds are becoming darker. Satan deceives men into believing their dark deeds will not lead to condemnation and death, but Jesus declared, *"And this is the condemnation, that light is come into the world, and men loved darkness rather than light, because their deeds were evil" John 3:19(KJV).*

Jesus Christ is the light, the glory of God that came into the world but many have rejected Him because they love darkness and the evil deeds perpetrated in the darkness. There are times when an individual is so immersed in something it becomes normal to him. Others on the outside can see the terrible state of the individual but the individual himself is so bound he is unable to see the seriousness of his condition. Some people will actually try to convince you they are doing well when it is evident their lives are on a path of destruction. There has to be a strong spirit of delusion and deception by the Devil working in the person's life, fooling him into thinking he is free when he is actually bound. I know when I was living a lifestyle of sin which included drinking, drug dealing and fornication, I was so trapped and deceived that on many occasions I tried to justify the wrong I did when others tried to get me to take a look at myself.

So often we are busy looking at the faults of others that we fail to discern the chains that are holding us captive. The loss of my freedom through the prison sentence I was given in England forced me to begin to take an introspective look at my life. Being shut up far away from my wife and children in a damp isolated cell, far removed from the Moet champagne, the gold and diamond jewelry, which created a façade of success; I was able to see the real person whose identity was masked by the trappings of the trinkets acquired by years of self-indulgence in sin. When I saw the "real me" and the chains of rebellion that had me bound and led me to the English prison, I was horrified to say the least, and knew I needed a transformation fast.

I knew I could not transform myself, and was powerless to break those chains because I was placed behind prison bars after being transported with real chains called handcuffs on my wrists. The handcuffs and the barbed wire prison wall was the tangible manifestation of the fruit of a life that was bound by sinful chains. On the streets, I lived a life of total deception because I thought I was a player, a mover and a shaker. There was always someone there to pat the drug dealer on the back and make him think he was the man. The people who love us and are trying to warn us of impending destruction are looked upon as nuisances but when tragedy comes we realize who really had our best interest at heart. I wore expensive gold chains and diamond rings on the streets but they could not mask the chains the Devil had around my mind. When I was arrested the gold chains were replaced by silver bracelets called hand cuffs, gold bars were replaced by prison bars.

It is unfortunate that it took the manacle and shackle of the law for me to come to the realization that life outside of Christ is futile, money earned from sinful actions will take wings and fly away. On the streets, I had thousands of dollars at my disposal but in prison I had to labor for pennies. The blinding of my mind and the deafening of my ears hindered me from seeing and hearing what the Lord was speaking to me through the various individuals He sent my way. The irony of it all is, my wife who was sleeping right next to me had the answer all the time but I refused to listen. If I had listened to my wife and others, prison would not have been the place of my epiphany, but thanks be to God for the Lord Jesus Christ who used my failures to show me a better way.

If God does not take delight in the death of the wicked, He sure does not take delight in the death and destruction of individuals who are deceived by the Devil. The person sitting in prison today or in some other situation bound with chains need not settle; they should allow the glorious light of the gospel of Christ to shine in that dark place. God is just a prayer of repentance away; it does not matter the thickness off the chain that has you bound; Christ can break any chain. The amazing thing about my prison sentence was the fact that God used the prison to free me; sounds like an oxymoron right? How can someone who is in prison be free? My physical body was in prison because of the crime I committed but through salvation Jesus freed my mind. When I was on the streets my body was free in the sense that I was not confined to a cell but my mind was imprisoned by the chains of a sinful lifestyle.

I remember when I was given the eight year prison sentence and returned to the place where I was remanded. One of the inmates asked me how it went in court and I told him I was sentenced to eight years; his jaw dropped and a pale look of sadness enveloped his face. Truthfully, I had peace because I knew the presence of the Lord was with me. Not long after, the same inmate beat his case and went home. One day I saw his co-defendant on the landing and he had tears in his eyes. When I asked him what happened he told me that his co-defendant had been murdered. I was stunned because I could see the look that was on his face when I told him about my sentence.

As I stood in front of the inmate with tears in his eyes, the thought came to my mind that I was in prison yet I had been freed by the righteous Judge, but his co-defendant was set free by an earthly judge but was now permanently bound with chains of darkness. The individual who was murdered after winning his case at trial was one of many that left prison and was killed shortly thereafter. They did not leave prison with a repentant heart so they went on the outside and resumed the lifestyles that had gotten them incarnated. God is no respecter of persons and I truly believe that prison should have been a wakeup call for them, but the problem was many of them had lengthy criminal records and had become anesthetized to the prison environment, not realizing that the arrest they experienced before their demise by death would be their last one. If you are reading these words from a prison or jail cell right now, it is not by chance or happen stance. God has orchestrated it so you could read it and come to a place of repentance if you are not saved.

TAKE A MOMENT RIGHT NOW AND REPENT OF YOUR SINS AND ASK JESUS TO COME INTO YOUR HEART AND BE THE LORD OF YOUR LIFE. IF YOU DO NOT KNOW HOW TO REPENT SIMPLY READ THE FOLLOWING SCRIPTURE AND DO WHAT IT SAYS WITH A SINCERE HEART.

"That if thou shalt confess with thy mouth the Lord Jesus, and shalt believe in thine heart that God hath raised him from the dead, thou shalt be saved. For with the heart man believeth unto righteousness; and with the mouth confession is made unto salvation" Romans 10:9-10 (KJV). Do not put it off until tomorrow because tomorrow is not promised to you. *"Harden not your heart, as in the provocation, and as in the day of temptation in the wilderness"* Psalm 95:8(KJV).

Sinners may feel like they have time on their side because they are oblivious to the fact that sin is like a noose made out of steel, and the Devil is tightening the noose and slowly suffocating the life out of them. Many people have heard a gospel message or a witness calling them to repentance and did not heed the call because they thought they had time. If the dead could speak I am sure they would send an immediate warning to their loved ones to repent quickly and avert the destruction that is coming to all people outside the ark of safety in Jesus Christ. I marvel when I watch documentaries on the lives of some of the most notorious so called gangsters and drug dealers; they flood their communities with drugs, murder and mayhem but hand out turkey's at Thanksgiving, and give toys to tots. Because of their generosity people in the community hail these individuals as heroes instead of zeroes.

A hero does not do things to destroy the community he does things to build the community. I was so self-centered in my pursuit of the things that pleased my flesh until I was unable to see the effect my lifestyle had on the community myself and my family. Prison was my wake up call and that wake up call was reinforced when I came to the realization that I was a failure as a husband and father. This realization was more difficult to deal with than the actual confinement of prison. Marcus Garvey said, *"a man never knows himself until his back is against a wall."* When a person's back is against the wall he realizes that he can go no further in the condition he is in; for me it was the prison wall. I came to the understanding that transformation could only come through a changing of my thought process.

The manner in which I thought and acted in the streets led me back to the prison wall and I knew that I did not want that to be the end of my story. I did not want my gravestone to read, here buried is an ex-con, a drug dealer and wine bibber. In order for my story to have a more positive ending, I had to have the blinders taken off, the chains cut and the bands loosed; I had to come to the realization that I had lived a life of total deception and blindness to that point. What started out as a time of hustling to make money to live a life based around the flesh quickly became a life of bondage which was leading to death. The Devil will show us the glitz and the glamour of sin but he will not let us see the death and destruction that is lurking beneath it. He is a master illusionist so he uses all types of schemes and tricks to blind the sinner, making them think they can lead a good life outside of Jesus Christ.

The trappings of sin can be pleasant to the lustful eye causing the individual to be blind and ignorant of the dangers they bring. Deceived individuals will think God is answering their prayers because instead of punishment for their lifestyles, there is a season of prosperity. The Devil will use those seasons to lull his victims into a false sense of security. If God answered our prayers and blessed us in our sin, why would there be a sense of urgency to repent and cease from ungodly activity. All that glitters is not gold, and all that sparkle is not a diamond. In describing the temptation of Jesus by the Devil the Bible declares, *"Again, the devil taketh him up into an exceeding high mountain, and sheweth him all the kingdoms of the world, and the glory of them; And saith unto him, All these things will I give thee, if thou wilt fall down and worship me" Matthew 4:8-9(KJV).*

Have you ever noticed some celebrities when they receive an award? Some of them will say, *"I would like to thank god or I would like to thank the lord."* What god and what lord are they thanking? The god of this age and the lord of the flies can take people to high mountains of musical celebrity, sports celebrity, and theatrical celebrity and show them the glory of those things and tell them they can have them if they are willing to worship him. The same Devil that tempted Jesus in the wilderness with empty promises of glory will also tempt believers with trappings of ministerial wealth and success if they compromise the gospel and bow to him in worship. When this occurs they are blinded with the trappings of success and begin to preach a gospel that does not threaten the kingdom of darkness and does not cut the chains holding people bound.

Paul told the Corinthian Church, *"But if our gospel be hid, it is hid to them that are lost: in whom the god of this world hath blinded the minds of them which believe not, lest the light of the glorious gospel of Christ, who is the image of God, should shine unto them" 2 Corinthians 4:4(KJV).* I truly believe that many people would repent and call on the name of Jesus for salvation if they could see the end result of a sinful life outside of Jesus Christ; unfortunately many will not realize until it is too late. Allow me to give you an example how blind my mind was when I fell for the Devil's deceit. When I was preparing to make the trip to England I could not find my passport. I practically tore the house apart looking for it; when I could not find it I began to accuse my wife of hiding it.

My wife told me that God did not want me to go to England so when I found the passport I held it up in her face and said, *"see, God wants me to go because I found my passport;"* That would be the last time I would see my precious wife until three years later. There are untold individuals today sitting in prisons cells, buried in graves, bound to wheelchairs or bedridden because they refused to heed the warnings of the people around them who could discern the fact that their actions were leading them down a path of death and de-struction. God placed people around them like solitary diamonds to bring them out of the place of bondage, but they find themselves dwelling in a dry land because of an inability or a refusal to receive and act upon the warnings they received. They have the chains of blindness around their mind; they are so steeped in deception they refuse to allow the light of the gospel to shine. These are not neces-sarily people who are going to commit some heinous act like murder, rape, or assault; it can be an individual whose heart is full of pride and arrogance which leads him to believe he does not need God.

The irony is this; everyone is subservient to something or some-one. The person who has become aloof and filled with a spirit of arrogance may surround themselves with a bunch of yes men who are unwilling or afraid to tell them their train is about to derail. Over the years many powerful men and women of God have fallen into disgrace because issues in their lives were overshadowed by their swift rise to religious fame and fortune. When David took the wife of Uriah as his wife after sending Uriah to the front of the battlefield to die, there was a Nathan in his life to bring him to a place of accountability for his actions. David was able to repent and get himself back in right standing with God.

Unlike some of the modern day leaders who lack true con-trition, David did not try to justify his sin with excuses; he took responsibility for his actions and asked God to, *"create a clean heart and renew a right spirit in him" Psalm 51:10(KJV).* After ask-ing for a clean heart and a right spirit David went on to say, *"Cast me not away from thy presence; and take not thy holy spirit from me. Restore unto me the joy of thy salvation; and uphold me with thy free spirit. Then will I teach transgressors thy ways; and sinners shall be converted unto thee" Psalm 51:11-13(KJV).* When the Lord restores us we must have a desire to teach transgressors his ways so they can be converted. He does not restore us so we can become Pentecostal charismatic celebrities; he does it so we can impact the world through righteousness.

How different was David from some of the televangelist of today. They spend time and a great deal of advertising money trying to convince us if we send in a large seed we will prosper financially and materially. They have messages that try to teach us how to be wealthy and successful; David's desire was to teach transgressors and to see sinners converted. If he was bound by the chains of pride and arrogance he would not have cried out to God in repentance. When you see leaders falling from the lofty heights upon which they are perched, they have had many warnings and near misses that should have led them to a place of repentance and a turning away from that which is vain to that which is holy. When I was given the chance to go on Christian television, I thought I was going to advertise my books, but the precious Holy Spirit spoke to my heart and told me to share my testimony.

Wow, a chance to be on Christian television and instead of discussing the revelation in my book, He told me to look in the camera and let the people know I was a drug dealer, fornicator and adulterer, but Jesus had washed and cleansed me of my unrighteousness when I came to myself and repented like the prodigal son. I had to let the viewer's know that Jesus forgave me and He was willing to forgive them if they were willing to repent and ask for forgiveness. God, our Father in heaven, is ready and willing to forgive us of our sins and trespasses but unfortunately, many people are walking around bound with a spirit of condemnation and chained with a spirit of unforgiveness. They live tormented lives and carry unforgiveness, hurt and pain from the past for many years.

The failure to forgive keeps the person trapped or chained to a past event that causes a great deal of pain. Many have suppressed such pain and think they are over it because it is buried deep within their subconscious; they are oblivious to the fact that the unresolved situation has an effect on how they deal with people in the present.

In their minds they think they are free but others can see there is some deep seated unresolved issues that influence the way they react to current situations. A person who suffered rape or molestation in the past can become cold and rigid when in a relationship with someone whom they love or someone who loves them. God's word is a chain cutting tool that can bring deliverance to each case but the person must receive His word and allow it to cut the chain.

The process of being freed from the chain may mean the person has to swallow their pride, come down from their lofty perch, and crucify their flesh by facing the person or the situation that has caused them to be bound. The process is not easy but it is necessary if deliverance is to come. As good and beneficial as advice is, it is easier to give it than to receive it. It is easy for us to see the chains that have others bound and very easy for us to give them advice on how to be free; but it is not as easy when it is our time to receive and act upon advice, especially when it challenges our flesh. As mentioned previously, the person with chains of unforgiveness usually has a spirit of pride. Pride is one of the major chains or weapons of mass destruction used by the Devil to keep people bound. *"Pride goeth before destruction, and an haughty spirit before a fall" Proverbs 16:18(KJV).*

Whenever there is destruction or a fall, there is pride and a haughty spirit present. Before the person falls and is destroyed there is usually a word of warning. Pride will keep us from listening to good advice from others because we feel we have arrived at a place where we do not need advice. Pride not only blinds the eyes but it clogs the ears and when the ears are clogged balance is affected; once balance is affected falling is inevitable and with the fall comes destruction. The word of God comes to clean out our eyes and ears so we can see, hear and have a life of balance. Jesus told His disciples they were clean through the words He spoke to them. They were clean because they allowed His words to penetrate into the places that needed cleansing; they allowed His words to cut away chains that held them bound to uncleanness.

Jesus' words to the individual bound with the chain of pride are these, *"Come unto me, all ye that labour and are heavy laden, and I will give you rest. Take my yoke upon you, and learn of me; for I am meek and lowly in heart: ye shall find rest unto your souls. For my yoke is easy, and my burden is light" Matthew 11:28-30(KJV).* Many people we come across in our daily lives are heavy laden and burdened with cumbersome chains; these individuals have no rest because they are worn out mentally from dragging around burdens they were not created to carry. Jesus desires to teach them how to be meek and lowly in heart so they can find rest for their burdened minds. When a person is willing to lose their false pride and be yoked with the mind of Jesus they will feel free. Jesus is able to sever every chain of burden that has the mind feeling weary and tired.

True peace and rest comes to the mind that is resting in Him. Worldly solutions are like a Band Aid; they cover the sore but do not treat the root of the problem. Jesus does not treat symptoms He gets to the root of the problem and cuts away the things that are causing us to feel heavy laden. I believe the Devil's greatest weapon or chain is the spirit of deception. People who are deceived have blinders on and cannot see the root of the deception. Since Satan is the god of this age and the ruler of the world's carnal system, he knows what to do to keep people trapped in darkness yet believing they are actually good people. There are many who think self-righteous acts and good deeds will justify them in the sight of God.

There are also many who think because they have not committed a major sin and have tried to live a moral life, that they are alright in the sight of God, *"But we are all as an unclean thing, and all our righteousnesses are as filthy rags; and we all do fade as a leaf; and our iniquities, like the wind, have taken us away" Isaiah 64:6(KJV).* Jesus Christ is the only one who can impute the righteousness of God to us, but first we must come to the realization of the wretchedness of life without Christ. Some men will give heed and repent while others sear their consciences and continue to live in sin. I am always intrigued by some people's response when a tragedy hits home or close to it. Individuals will often ask the question, *"Why did God allow it to happen?"*

The world's system is under the bondage and curse of sin and the fruit of that sin is death and destruction. The Bible lets us know that the sun shines on the just and the unjust and I believe that the same manner tragedy touches the just and the unjust; the difference is, the just have peace in the midst of the storm because they know that in this world they will have tribulation but Jesus Christ has overcome the world. The Bible tells believers to be in the world but not of the world. We live in the world so our lives are affected by the things, which befall the world but we do not process and deal with those things in the manner that the people of the world do. Disciples do not allow themselves to be bound by the chains of flesh that keep the children of the world bound. Jesus Christ sets His disciples in the world as solitary diamonds that have been cut and polished, living according to the word of God and shining with the light of His glory. They are here to be lights shining in a dark place. Their lives are to be distinct and different from the lives of the children of darkness.

Disciples are not here to fit in or to be friends of the world because friends of the world are enemies of God. When we are walking in the light of the Lord and being led by Holy Spirit, it is not difficult to discern people who have a form of Godliness while denying the power. The power of God comes through the Holy Spirit and allows us to resist the temptations and encroachment of the world's carnal system upon our lives. Some people try to live as close to the world as possible while easing their consciences with religious activity; God is not mocked, a man can only reap from what he has sown. Our light has to shine so blind men can see their need for a Savior. Blind men seeing may sound like a contradiction but it is not. Satan, the god of this age, has blinded their eyes with chains of deception but the God of grace and mercy never leaves them completely void of an opportunity to repent and call on Him.

Somewhere along the way before they become totally blind and lost through a reprobate mind, He allows them multiple opportunities for repentance. When the person gets to a place or a state of complete blindness, he has rejected all the God given opportunities. This is the reason why disciples are set in the earth by God as cut and polished solitary diamonds that must be steadfast in spreading the gospel. We are to be living epistles to be read by all men; they must have the opportunity to see Christ in us - the hope of glory - so they can make a decision before it is too late. We have not been cut and polished, only to be set in a trophy case called the local church. He has cut and polished us to use us as His instrument of deliverance or His chain cutting tool. Those who do not allow God to bring them out of the bondage of sin by breaking the chains that hold them bound will dwell in a dry land.

These individuals are the people the psalmist describe as the rebellious dwelling in a dry land. The Bible describes rebellion as the sin of witchcraft. When an individual refuses to accept Jesus Christ in the pardoning of their sin they will not have access to the power of God's Holy Spirit. He is the river of living water that quenches the thirsty soul. The pleasures of sin for a season is so enticing people would rather receive the temporary euphoria they bring rather than surrender to Jesus and enjoy an eternity of refreshing in the presence of God. These individuals are so consumed by those pleasures they are unaware of the drought that is on the other side. It is one thing to go through seasons of a dry land but it is a completely different thing to have to dwell in a land that is dry.

A dry land is symbolic of being in a place where the Spirit of God does not reside; if the Spirit of God is not residing in a place it means that the spirit of the anti-Christ is there, and that must be a horrible place. Our lives on this earth in a physical body are temporal but our lives after death will be a permanent one. It makes more sense to keep our lives surrendered to God so He can get glory out of us in this life and the life to come. The person with the surrendered life will dwell in a land that is filled with His presence, which is similar to a place where there is fullness of joy. The person living in rebellion is confined to a dry land, constantly employing human ingenuity and self-will to alleviate the dryness of their condition. As foresaid, the pleasures of sin and rebellion only last for a season, and though some seasons are long, no season last forever, and that is why they are called seasons. With the understanding that seasons are temporal is it not more wise or sensible to spend the seasons of our lives growing in the things of the Holy Spirit and not the things of the flesh.

Chapter 9
Kingdom Promotion Comes Through Death

*It may seem contradictory to use the word promotion and the
word death in the same sentence but an understanding of the
Kingdom of God and the death of the flesh gives us understanding
of why one is necessary for the other to be manifested.*

W hether in school or on the job, human beings have a desire to be promoted from one grade or position to another especially when they have fulfilled certain criteria. This feeling should be no different when it comes to our relationship with God. In the secular realm, job promotion usually has amenities attached to it like a pay increase, more vacation and in some instances a managerial or supervisory title with responsibility over other employees. In kingdom promotion, the amenities are more righteousness, more peace and more joy in the Holy Ghost. Unlike the secular realm, kingdom promotion for a disciple means being a greater servant radiating more of God's glory. The disciple must understand that the paradigm used in the secular realm to achieve promotion and its amenities, may be problematic when it comes to kingdom promotion. Here is what I mean, in the secular realm an individual may be driven to succeed because of pride, ambition and hard work. These attributes may cause him/her to step on some people on their way up, and may entice them to compromise their morality or integrity in pursuit of power through promotion. Fortunately, unlike man, God will not promote a disciple if their motives are not pure. Men and women can promote us in the church but only God can promote us in the kingdom. Since no flesh can glory in His presence, anything done from a fleshly, carnal perspective will not produce kingdom promotion.

KINGDOM PROMOTION HAS A GREAT DEAL TO DO WITH THE GLORY. IN ORDER TO HAVE THE VALUE, SHINE AND THE GLORY OF A BEAUTIFUL PRECIOUS DIAMOND, THE DISCIPLE HAS TO COME TO A PLACE WHERE PROMOTION FOR SELF GRATIFICATION AND ACCOLADES FROM PEOPLE IS NOT IN HIS HEART.

Show me someone whom God has promoted and I will show you someone walking in a greater level of death of the flesh. Much of what is passed off today as Godly success is nothing more than charismatic success succored through human will and intellect. God desires to prepare and promote His children to operate in a kingdom realm but His children must embrace the process of death of the flesh. When the Lord saved me in prison I delighted in telling other inmates about Him. My cell turned into a place of weekly Bible study and I witnessed the transforming power in the word of God when it is applied in the life of a sinner. I had no dreams or ambitions of preaching in a pulpit, on television or radio. I never thought about offerings or any other financial gain. As a matter of fact, I did not consider myself a preacher; I was just someone who loved Jesus and wanted to tell as many people as I could about Him.

When I was released from prison I was full of joy. I found myself even more joyful when given the opportunity to witness on the streets, in Rikers Island Prison and in Elmcor Drug and Alcohol Rehabilitation Center. After I joined a local church I started to see the glamour and the monetary aspects of ministering. I was given a chance to preach and it really felt good especially when there was a positive response for the congregants. I did not receive a love offering at that time because I was a member and I was fine with that because I just loved sharing the word of God. As I started visiting end evangelizing in other churches I observed how people doted over preachers, the excessiveness in attire and the abuse during the collection of the offering. I knew I never wanted to get to a place where I used trickery to get money out of God's people. When I started watching Christian television and saw the large crowds being ministered to by the televangelist I was in awe. I would not say I had a desire to be like them but I definitely had a desire to travel and minister full time.

I was often told that I would not be considered a success if I did not preach a certain way, wear certain styles of clothing and minister before large audiences, but my motivation was not wealth and prestige. However, somewhere along the way a seed was planted in me and it needed to die. I thought I was ready to be promoted to full time evangelism and stepped out only to fall flat on my face (sometimes we can have motives and agendas deep down in us that we are not fully aware of). The Lord spoke to my heart and let me know that I needed to work and help my wife raise our children before I tried to evangelize the world. Many doors seemed to close around me but it was God who allowed it because He was doing a work on the inside of me.

When the time drew near for God to elevate me to a full time position of traveling with His gospel, he had my friend and brother in the Lord Prophet Emmanuel Haniah to call and pray for me on a regular basis. On one occasion when he called me he began to discuss death and dying to self. When he talked about death and the flesh I had to begin to take a serious look at myself and my approach to ministry. I was horrified by what I saw and realized the word on death was for me. I saw things in my walk with God that I knew came from my soul and not from God. In my heart I had to come to a place where I was willing to minister the gospel of Jesus Christ even if it meant no one would ever remember me or I would speak to small audiences with no great financial compensation. I could not judge myself by the success of other ministers, but by whether or not God was pleased with me.

In my heart, I knew power and influence gained through looks and talent, not saying that I have either, was corrupting. I was also cognizant of the fact that the process of dying to self was a daily process because the moment I did not surrender to the process self-will would take root and lead me on a path not pleasing to God. The irony is, a path that is not pleasing to God can appear to be successful to the world in terms of the glitz and the glamour but if God is not pleased the path will lead to shame and disgrace. This reminds me so much of a diamond; to the world you look so good but when you get in private and take a closer look at yourself you can see you're not really a diamond but a fake. This is why many celebrities are miserable. To the world they have everything but when those celebrities get home they are depressed and turning to drugs for relief.

There are great men and women of God who started out with a pure heart but became corrupt when money and prestige came to them. The landscape of life is littered with a litany of men and women who had the wealth and prestige of an international ministry but is now in the hall of shame because some seed of self was planted along the path and was allowed to grow until it produced the fruit of shame and degradation. The popular saying *"The bigger they are the harder they fall"* is why no one should be envious of the success of another because we don't know what the person had to do to get the position and how much it is costing them to maintain it. I knew there were times in my life when I saw my ministerial biological clock ticking and became nervous because I felt I was getting older and was not where I thought I should be in ministry. I remember being so frustrated one day *"I told my wife that I had either missed God or was not called to preach."* I felt that way because I had not received any invitations for speaking engagements. My wife replied *"be patient and remember how old Moses was when God called him."* Her response did not comfort me because I realized people were not living as long as they did in Moses' day. Although I had a pure desire to minister that desire was negatively affected by a misguided notion and a paradigm of successful ministry based on the size of the crowd, and the trappings of success. God knew this because God looks at the heart of man.

Remember, all that glistens and shines is not a genuine diamond and all that appears successful in ministry is not for the glory of God. Kingdom promotion does not necessarily mean a person will have outward trappings of wealth and prestige; it means God is pleased and the person is at a place where they are not seeking to be seen or heard but seeking to have Christ seen and heard in and through them. The humblest person in Christ can have a seed of pride planted in them if they let their guard down; so it behooves us all to search our hearts daily to see if something ungodly has been planted and needs to die. God did not say the serpent was more subtle than any beast of the field for nothing.

When the Devil or his minions are planting a seed of deception they do it with subtlety. One of the saddest things to witness is a person in Christ who is filled with pride, arrogance and self-deception but unable to discern it. Every one of us came into this world with the root of self in us and that is why when we are born again in Christ, God takes us through the furnace of affliction to burn away everything out of us that defiles and pollutes the temple. Each person will have to decide how much of God's Spirit they desire in their temple. The level of indwelling of His Spirit is correlated to the level of death, by heat, pressure, volcanic eruptions, cutting and polishing that come through fiery trials.

KINGDOM PROMOTION TAKES THE DISCIPLE TO THE THIRD DIMENSION WHICH IS PARADISE, BUT KINGDOM PROMOTION CAN ONLY BE ATTAINED THROUGH THE DEATH OF FLESH.

There must be a willing recognition on the part of the disciple that no good thing dwells in the flesh. There is nothing good dwelling in the flesh because it is the center of all ungodly desires. It is the part of us that delights in sinful things and not the things of God. It does not desire the things of God and never will. There is nothing a person can do to make the flesh desirable to God; it is an enemy of God and will always be. We can attempt to mask the flesh behind earthly success but eventually it will be exposed because it is a stench in the nostrils of God. Over the years many successful men of God who were considered paragons of virtue have fallen to places of ill repute to the shock and dismay of their followers.

We must never forget that men's feet are made of fragile clay and we must pray for the men and women of God because the devil is out to kill, steal and destroy. Unfortunately, at times we give the enemy the ammunition he needs to bring us down. We must not be mesmerized by the bright lights and the charisma of leaders in the spotlight; they are human beings like you and I and if those leaders are not careful they will be lead into temptation. My wife used to work in the home of a great man and woman of God and was able to witness many of their human frailties; she prayed for them constantly because she realized they along with their children, were targets of the enemies attacks because of the position they held in the body of Christ. The colossal fall of a man or woman of God does not happen overnight. Somewhere along the way they refused to heed God's warning signals. Many allowed success to blind and deafen them to the cliff which awaited them.

Samson is a biblical example of an individual with great potential but was brought down by his enemies because of a lack of self-control in terms of his sexuality, arrogance and a trust in his own strength. Because of God's grace his hair which was an emblem of his strength began to grow again after it had been cut by Delilah and his strength returned, allowing him to destroy his enemies, but he died with them. God is full of grace and mercy and will restore us when we have fallen but it is better to listen to Him and avoid falling. As we desire to go higher in God which sometimes manifest itself in greater prestige and success in the secular realm, we must be aware of the fact that if there is unconfessed sin or some fleshly desire that we are feeding, the fall will be harder and greater.

The devil could not bring Jesus down because there was no opening in Him for the enemy to place a hook and pull Him down. He was full of God's spirit and had a total desire to do His will. A disciple can experience some of God's presence before total deliverance from the carnal nature, but to walk fully in a kingdom paradigm will require complete death of the flesh. It is an extremely difficult but not an impossible process. We have the word of God as our witness and our evidence to show us examples of individuals like Paul who yielded to the process of purification through the furnace of affliction for flesh annihilation so he could attain the experience of the third dimension. A mere religious experience will not take us there; church membership will not take us there, good works will not take us there. Jesus Christ is the only one who can give us entrance to that dimension. It is a spiritual realm that is attained by disciples who are walking in the Spirit.

I cannot emphasize enough how essential it is for disciples of Christ to search our hearts daily to see if there is any ungodly thing like pride on the throne. Pride is like an octopus with a multitude of tentacles such as un-forgiveness, bitterness, anger, rage and much more. *"When pride cometh, then cometh shame: but with the lowly is wisdom" Proverbs 11:2(KJV).* Pride brought down Lucifer and caused him to become Satan a hideous creature, and pride in a human heart will bring the person down to a terrible and hideous state. *"Pride goeth before destruction, and an haughty spirit before a fall. Better it is to be of an humble spirit with the lowly, than to divide the spoil with the proud Proverbs 16:18-19(KJV).*

Jesus told His disciples that He saw Satan as lightening fall from heaven, the swift fall occurred because Satan was heavy laden with pride. Jesus told the disciples about the fall of Satan because they were excited about demons being subject to them in His name. He told them to rejoice that their names were written in heaven. They walked with Jesus; demons were subject to them because He gave them power to tread upon serpents and scorpions and over all the power of the enemy, but heaven was the thing that should bring joy to the hearts of His disciples. Gifts and callings can cause a person to be puffed up with pride, but keep in mind; gifts and callings are without repentance. A person can operate in great gifts and have a heart full of pride and be un-repentant. It is imperative that we keep our eyes on the prize which is heaven. There will be people who stand before Jesus and hear the words, *"depart from me you workers of iniquity, I knew not."* They will say, *"Lord, Lord, have we not prophesied in thy name? and in thy name have cast out devils? And in thy name done many wonderful works?" Matthew 7:23(KJV)*

It would appear that an individual who walks in that level of anointing would be a lock for heaven, but obviously something was missing in terms of their motivation and obedience to what Jesus called them to do. I believe there was no intimacy with Him in terms of dedication and that is why they heard, *"I knew you not."* The spirit of deception is very subtle so believers and disciples must not allow gifting and callings to deceive them into thinking because they prophesy in the name of Jesus and cast out devils, they are in good standing with Him. *"Examine yourselves, whether ye be in the faith; prove your own selves. Know ye not your own selves, how that Jesus Christ is in you, except ye be reprobates"? 2 Corinthians 13:5(KJV)*

According to Paul we must examine ourselves to see if we are in the faith, meaning are we operating according to faith in Jesus? Jesus never did anything to be seen of men; He only did the things which pleased His Father. The Holy Spirit never speaks of Himself but speaks of Jesus. When the Father speaks of the Son He says, *"This is my beloved Son, in whom I am well pleased" Matthew 3:17(KJV).* Some people avoid self-examination because they are afraid of what they may find. It is better to do true self-examination and see the things of the flesh which displease our Father and grieve the Holy Spirit rather than operate in a state of self-deception and fall into a reprobate state. Charismatic gifts may blind people to the spirit of pride and arrogance operating in the preacher but Jesus is not deceived; He sees beyond the gifts and examines the heart of the individual.

I believe the Lord desires His disciples to come to revelations and visions of His glory while we are here on the earth, but we must examine ourselves daily to see the carnal thoughts words and deeds in our hearts and ask the Lord to burn them out. *"Verily, verily, I say unto you, Except a corn of wheat fall into the ground and die, it abideth alone: but if it die, it bringeth forth much fruit. He that loveth his life shall lose it; and he that hateth his life in this world shall keep it unto life eternal" John 12:24-25(KJV).* When we are willing to die to self and lose our life for Christ in this world our lives can produce much fruit for Him. Just like when God's fire burns away the dross from our hearts for fruit production, the process is synonymous to the extreme heat and pressure needed to create a diamond.

There are many atoms of carbon beneath the earth's surface but not all of them become a rock forming diamond; only the ones in the mantle which can endure and persevere; the diamond survives the volcanic eruptions in-order to get to the earth's surface to be mined, cut and polished. The diamond with the proper cut and polish will reflect the greatest amount of light and fetch the highest price. There are many believers in Christ, but only the ones willing to endure extreme heat and pressure will have the privilege to have Christ, the solid rock, formed in them. Only the ones sturdy enough to endure the volcanic eruptions will have Christ come to the surface in them, only the ones willing to be cut and polished to remove the rough edges will radiate God's glory and walk in Kingdom authority.

PART FOUR

Chapter 10
The Hope of Glory

After countless tests and trails it is every disciple's goal to be without spot or wrinkle; like a flawless diamond, waiting with HOPE and expectancy to see our Lord and Savior Jesus Christ.

*T*he Hope Diamond is considered the most famous diamond in the world. It is a 45.2-carat deep-blue diamond housed in the Smithsonian Natural History Museum in Washington, D.C. The original diamond weighed a little over 112 carats before jewelers cut the stone down. It was cut into a round brilliant shape with additional facets along the pavilion or base of the stone, to bring out the rich sparkle and color of the diamond. After cut, color is generally considered the second most important characteristic when selecting a diamond. This is because the human eye tends to detect a diamond's sparkle (light performance) first, and color second. In order to get more beauty and brilliance, the Hope Diamond had to have some weight or carats cut off. Big is not always best. Any sacrifice undertaken to get the most beauty and value out of an object or a person is worthwhile. Jesus Christ made the ultimate sacrifice to get beauty and value out of those God has redeemed.

"The Hope Diamond has been described as the most famous diamond in the world; and is said to be the second most-visited artwork in the world, after the Mona Lisa. It is set into a white diamond necklace which includes 61 other diamonds. Where am I going with this? Diamonds do not keep company with cubic zirconia or other fake gems. Diamonds must be paired with other diamonds that have gone through the process of extreme heat, pressure, cutting and polishing. There is a familiar cliché, *"Birds of a feather flock together."* Another is *"Eagles do not hang around with chickens and buzzards"*.

A diamond of the caliber of the Hope Diamond has to be surrounded by other high quality diamonds that will accentuate its
beauty. When I was younger my mother gave me several wise nug-
gets , *"if you lay down with dogs you will get up with flees; show me
your company and I will tell you who you are; the apple does not fall
far from the tree; what drops off the head drops on the shoulders."* I
never understood the fullness of her wise sayings until I ignored
them and had to deal with the consequences. When Jesus Christ
the hope of glory came to dwell on the inside of me through the
Spirit, I gained the wisdom to stop keeping company with chickens and buzzards and started associating with people who were
kingdom minded. In the world I was governed by my carnal nature
and attracted people who were carnal and not spiritually minded.
Relationships built on carnality have very few lasting benefits, because they are not built on a solid foundation. When I ended up in
prison the fair weather friends disappeared and my only hope of
survival and support system was the Lord Jesus Christ; He became
the friend that stuck closer than a brother so I placed my hope and
trust in Him.

When the word hope is used in the Bible the meaning and
the connotation is different from the way it is used in English.
A student may hope to get a good grade on a math test; or after
filling out a job application and going through an interview, hope
to become gainfully employed. There is a feeling of uncertainty
when the word hope is used in that manner. According to Random
House Webster's College Dictionary Hope is, *"the feeling that what
is wanted can be had or that events will turn out well."* Biblical hope
is more than a feeling, it is an assurance. When Paul wrote to the
Colossians informing them that Christ in them was the hope of
glory, he was giving them some assurance.

The Greek word *elpis* is used for hope and it comes from the
word *elpo* which means, *to anticipate, usually with pleasure; expectation confidence or faith.* The children of God have a blessed assurance that His promises will be fulfilled in their lives because their
hope is not based on what may or may not happen but on Christ
the solid rock. Worldly hope can leave a person feeling anxious

and nervous, but hope in God leaves His children with a feeling of confidence and assurance. No matter what the circumstance or situation, a child of God must have confidence and assurance that God is able to perform His word. Fear and nervousness is a sign the believer is not trusting and hoping in Father God. *"Hope deferred maketh the heart sick: but when the desire cometh it is a tree of life" Proverbs 13:12(KJV)*.

The Hebrew word for hope there is *towcheleth* (pronounced *to-kheh-leth*); it comes from the word *yachal* which means, *to wait with expectation, to be patient, to trust*. Waiting can be challenging especially if the wait has been long. A woman waiting to be married can become nervous when she hears her biological clock ticking and there are no qualified suitors for her hand in marriage on the horizon. The question is, will she wait with confidence in God or will she take matters into her own hands, making forays into the flesh in an attempt to secure matrimony? When the enemy tries to place doubt, fear and anxiety in her mind if she does not focus and place her trust and confidence in God she will get a "Jack-az" instead of her "Boaz". The Hope Diamond has been described as having a dark blue color; it also emits a red glow. When it is exposed to short-wave ultraviolet light, it produces brilliant red phosphorescence (glow in the dark effect) that persists for some time after the light source has been switched off.

The red glow helps scientists fingerprint blue diamonds, allowing them to tell the real ones from the artificial. Blue and red are significant colors in the Bible.

SCIENTISTS ARE AIDED IN DETERMINING WHICH BLUE DIAMONDS ARE AUTHENTIC AND WHICH ARE FAKE BY THE RED GLOW THEY EMIT. BORN AGAIN BELIEVERS HAVE A SPIRITUAL RED GLOW BECAUSE THEY HAVE BEEN WASHED IN THE BLOOD OF JESUS CHRIST AND FILLED WITH HIS SPIRIT.

Redemption from sin and salvation cannot be received unless the sinner is washed in the blood of the Lamb. The blood of Jesus, the Lamb of God is the only hope a sinner has to be cleansed and reconciled to God. *"And almost all things are by the law purged with blood; and without shedding of blood is no remission" Hebrews 9:22(KJV).* Blood gives life to the flesh of every creature so when sin entered the world and death by sin, every creature needed a blood transfusion to avoid death and eternal separation from God. The transfusion could not come through a contaminated vessel so God sent Jesus as a Lamb without spot or blemish to provide the pure blood needed to expiate our sin. People can talk about God and participate in religious practices but their only hope for salvation is cleansing through the blood of the Lamb. If a person is not emitting a red glow like the priceless Hope Diamond then they are not an authentic child of God. The blood of Jesus allows a sinner to pass from death to eternal life.

When God decided it was time to deliver the Israelites from Egyptian bondage, he told Moses to, *"Speak ye unto all the congregation of Israel, saying, in the tenth day of this month they shall take to them every man a lamb, according to the house of their fathers, a lamb for an house" Exodus 12:3(KJV).*

When bringing deliverance every house needs a lamb. Israel was to take a lamb on the tenth day. Earlier I made reference to the M.O.H.S scale used to measure the sturdiness of gemstones and the fact that diamonds rate ten out of ten. The diamond disciple of Christ the Lamb will one day be a perfect ten because all impurities will be washed away by His blood. God told Moses, *"Your lamb shall be without blemish, a male of the first year: ye shall take it out from the sheep, or from the goats; And ye shall keep it up until the fourteenth day of the same month: and the whole assemble of the congregation of Israel shall kill it in the evening" Exodus 12:5-6(KJV).*

Christ the Lamb can perfect the sinner through His blood because He was without sin. The choosing of the lamb by the Israelites was a type or a foreshadowing of what was to come. The Israelites were instructed to take the blood from the slain lamb and strike it on the two side posts and on the upper door post of their houses. God instructed them that the slain lamb represented His Passover. *"For I will pass through the land of Egypt this night, and will smite all the firstborn in the land of Egypt, both man and beast; and against all the gods of Egypt I will execute judgment: I am the LORD. And the blood shall be to you for a token upon the houses where ye are: and when I see the blood, I will pass over you, and the plague shall not be upon you to destroy you, when I smite the land of Egypt" Exodus 12:12-13(KJV).*

Egypt is symbolic of the world's system that is under the bondage of sin and plagued with death. Sinners in the world's system are under the sin curse; they may be educated, wealthy and well-dressed but if they are not washed in the blood of Jesus they are under the curse. When God looks at each person in the world, the determining factor of whether or not that individual will go from death to eternal life is the blood of Jesus Christ, the Lamb over the door posts of their lives. In the New Testament or the New Covenant we see the manifestation of the Lamb of God who came to take away the sin of the world. While baptizing people in the Jordan River, *"The next day John seeth Jesus coming unto him, and saith, behold the Lamb of God, which taketh away the sin of the world" John 1:29(KJV).*

When the Passover was instituted according to the book of Exodus, the people were able to choose their own lamb. For the Exodus from sin and death for everyone in the world seeking salvation, God chose the Lamb. The Apostle John declared, *"And all that dwell upon the earth shall worship him, whose names are not written in the book of life of the Lamb slain from the foundation of the world. If any man have an ear, let him hear" Revelation 13:8-9(KJV).* Only those individuals who have been washed in the blood of the Lamb can have their names written in the book of life. The religions of the world cannot gain their adherents entrance and access into this book; the only hope is through the blood. All men have ears but only those who are able to hear the call of God through Jesus Christ and answer will have their names written in the book.

When the Lord Jesus Christ is ruling and reigning in the life of a disciple, he will radiate like the Hope Diamond. He will radiate with God's glory because where Christ dwells the glory of God will be manifested. The religions of the world offer a works based hope of salvation and a pseudo glory like the pseudo glory of a cubic zirconia, but that does not offer the eternal security one receives when he places his trust in the finished work of Jesus on the cross. If salvation was something money could buy the rich would live and the poor would die. God the Father gave the pure priceless blood of Jesus to redeem us. The only hope of glory for us is when Christ dwells in us; He is the conduit through which God's glory can flow into a vessel.

His dwelling place has to be a place of purity because the glory of God does not reside in polluted temples. The Apostle John wrote, *"Behold, what manner of love the Father hath bestowed upon us, that we should be called the sons of God: therefore the world knoweth us not, because it knew him not. Beloved, now are we the sons of God, and it doth not yet appear what we shall be: but we know that, when he shall appear, we shall be like him; for we shall see him as he is. And every man that hath this hope in him purifieth himself, even as he is pure" 1 John 3:1-3(KJV).* The fire, the heat, the cutting and the polishing will take us from where we are to a greater dimension in Him. When we gain an understanding of the process we have to go through to be like Him and to see Him; we understand that all the fiery trials we have to endure are worth it. There is no greater honor that can be bestowed on a person than to be washed in the Blood of Jesus, then to be purified and brought to a place where he can be like Him.

The immensity of God's love is awesome and unfathomable with the natural mind; His love opens the door for sinners to receive salvation and attain a place where they have the status, "Sons of God." Through the vicarious and atoning death of Jesus the sinner is transformed and receives the spirit of adoption whereby they have the right to call God Abba Father. The love of God causes Him to receive the most wretched vile sinner through the blood of Jesus. It would be enough if He reconciled the sinner and sent him on his way to live a good happy life, but God has so much love He adopts the redeemed person and makes them His son, what an awesome God. Many of the religions of the world describe their god as impersonal, but not so with the God and Father of our Lord

Jesus Christ, we love Him as a Father who cares for His children, not some distant being waiting to strike us when we mess up. He does not scare us into serving Him but loves us into fellowshipping with Him. Jesus came to reveal the heart of the Father to children who went astray through sin. If He was not a loving God He could have wiped out creation and started all over but instead of doing that He allowed Jesus to be the sacrifice in-order to restore us to a right relationship with Him. Jesus came as a Son and was mocked beaten and crucified, but stayed committed to His Father and to the assignment given to Him.

The sons of God will be mocked and persecuted for standing for righteousness because the world cannot understand; the world does not know our Father God in an intimate way He is known by His sons. Like Jesus the redeemed Sons of God must stay committed to the covenant relationship Jesus established for us with His blood. Our debt was paid by the priceless blood of Jesus and that is the evidence of the depth of God's love for His children. Many people throw the word love around and are very casual with its use; they love people who can love them in return and be a blessing for them, but God is not like man in that respect. God loved us and sent Jesus to die in our place while we were in a state where we deserved death instead of love. God's love is the foundation of our hope. We know that He cannot and will not fail us so we rest in Him knowing there is nothing that can separate us from His love. This confidence allows us to stand firm in Him when the world attempts to entice us into ungodliness.

God's sons do not entangle themselves in the affairs of this world; they are in the world but not of the world. They are not so heavenly minded that they are no earthly good; yet, they are cognizant of the fact they live in the world, they refuse to live like the world. Like the patriarch Abraham, they are pilgrims sojourning through this world, looking for a city which has foundations, and whose builder and maker is God" *Hebrews 11:10(KJV)*. The sons of God are able to withstand opposition in this world because their hope in God has firmly persuaded them Jesus has prepared a place for them with His Father that is much greater than the world in which they live. *"In my Father's house are many mansions: if it were not so, I would have told you. I go to prepare a place for you" John 14:2(KJV).* Can you imagine a house so large it contains many mansions? We have nothing here on earth to compare such a place with. The signs of the times tell us that the earth is heading for chaos and turmoil so it is awesome to know that the children of God have a place already prepared for them by Jesus. The earth as we know it is a temporal place but the prepared place is an eternal place. It is inconceivable to think that people would be so enamored with the pleasures of sin for a season they risk missing the opportunity to be in the prepared place. When they reject Jesus and the salvation He offers they in fact are rejecting an eternal home of glory for damnation.

The heroes in the hall of faith of Hebrews chapter 11 were willing to endure persecution rather than compromise their spiritual principles and integrity. They endured horrific treatment at the hands of persecutors because of their hope and trust in God. These heroes had to be the paradigm for modern day believers in terms of standing and trusting God under the threat of death. The sons of God must be strong in Him because fainting in the day of adversity shows little strength. Believers who faint will not have the title "Sons of God" bestowed on them. God's sons (male or female), are diamonds in the rough; people may see more rough than diamond when they are going through the process of purification but in time the dull rough edges will be cut away and they will shine with the radiance of the Lord. The purpose of the process is not for the diamond to be hid but for the beauty and splendor to be seen by those trapped in darkness. When they see the light of the sons of God it should give them hope for a future life with Christ. It should encourage them to desire to be loosed from the bondage of Satan so their lives can be transformed through Jesus.

The born again believer should never isolate themselves from unbelievers because it is through the light emanating from them that the unbeliever will cry out to God. God leaves His children in the earth so He can work in and through them in the earth. We know heaven is our goal and our home but while we are here on the earth we must fulfill the will of our Father God just like Jesus did. In every facet of our lives we are to be like Christ. He gave His life as ransom for many and so should we. It is important to understand that; Jesus Christ is the only one who can free a sinner bound with chains; therefore, when we surrender our lives, our carnal nature dies so He can live in us.

The most effective witness or chain cutter is the individual who witnesses from a place they have been delivered from. I send my books into the prisons because my testimony of deliverance from the English prison and the wretched lifestyle that led me there is a testimony that will resonate with individuals currently behind prison walls. Someone who has never served prison time can theorize what prison life is all about but someone who has actually served or is serving time in prison can give a factual representation of what it is actually like to be in prison. Whether it is a person in an actual prison or a person being held captive by some form of addiction, the testimony of a child of God who has been delivered through the power of His spirit will give the captive hope, that if God has done it for someone else He can do it for them. *"Let the redeemed of the Lord say so, whom he hath redeemed from the hand of the enemy"* Psalm 107:2 (KJV);

The redeemed are exhorted to speak forth the things the Lord has delivered them from so others can hear, receive hope and call upon His name. In the mouth of the redeemed is a mighty testimony of salvation and deliverance and it must be declared boldly. This brings glory to God and hope and encouragement to those seeking deliverance. The Hebrew word for redeemed is *ga'al (pronounced gaw-al)* and it refers to the Oriental law of kinship where a relative's property is bought back through the matrimony of his widow, as in the case of Boaz the kinsman redeemer who married Ruth after the death of her husband. It also means to *avenge* or to *ransom*.

Adam's rebellion caused sin to enter the world and death through sin; the entire human race came under the bondage of Satan because of His rebellion. Jesus Christ the last Adam is our near kinsman redeemer who took upon Himself the body of a human and shed His blood for us on the cross; He is the Bridegroom that is coming back for a bride without spot wrinkle or blemish. His bride is the redeemed whom He has washed in His blood, purified through the heat and pressure of the furnace of affliction, cut and polished. It is not His desire for anyone to be left out of the wedding feast and that is why He exhorts the redeemed of the Lord to, "*say so.*" A lost and dying world must see and hear the redeemed; they must see the light of His glory shining in and through them and they must hear His praises emanating from their mouth. His praises must come from the redeemed like a diamond cutting tool that cuts the chains and bring out those that are bound.

Chapter 11
The Third Dimension

As a diamond's three-dimensional structure gives it
its sturdiness, the disciple must have a revelation of
preparation to walk and dwell in the third dimension.

*E*very form of testing and trial by fire a disciple endures should be put in the perspective of preparation for God's glory. In other words, the disciple must have a three dimensional structure. The number three in scripture represents *resurrection, divine completeness*, and *perfection*. Therefore, the sinner must go through a process to become a believer and the believer must go through a process to ultimately become a disciple. A diamond is the hardest mineral on the planet and rates ten out of ten on the MOHS scale. This scale was developed by Friedrich Mohs in 1812. This is a relative scale of hardness from one to ten, as compared to other minerals.

A Diamond is the hardest mineral at ten and talc is the softest mineral at one. All other minerals are assigned hardness grades relative to these two minerals. A new convert in Christ is like a new born baby, soft as the mineral talc and needs the milk of the word to survive. Through the milk of the word and a series of testing, the baby Christian develops into a soldier who needs the meat of the word to become a warrior. The ultimate goal is to reach a rating of ten out of ten in terms of toughness and durability.

To earn a ten on the MOHS scale means the atoms of carbon had to endure the necessary heat and pressure in the mantle of the earth to become a diamond. Just as Friedrich Mohs used his name to develop the scale to grade the hardness of minerals, I would like to make an acronym out of the letters MOHS; that is *More Oil Holy Spirit.* Just like the heat applied to those atoms, to earn a ten the disciple of Christ has to be like an olive under a hydraulic press being crushed until it yields all its oil. The disciple's flesh has to be crushed until the oil of the Holy Spirit flows freely.

The third dimension or the third heaven is the dwelling place of the God Head. The believer who walks in the revelation of the third dimension of God's glory is sturdy and will not be tossed around by the storms of life. That revelation comes through an understanding of the trinity, how they work in and through the creation of the earth and the creation of man. The understanding of the trinity (Godhead) comes from the wisdom imparted through the Holy Spirit; hence the crushing of the flesh so the oil of God's wisdom can flow. God's desire is for His disciples to operate in the spirit of wisdom, understanding, counsel, might, knowledge and the fear of the LORD like Jesus did. For the disciple to have these characteristics and attributes of the Spirit, he must continually surrender his flesh to the process of death. As the flesh of the disciple is mortified, the Spirit will increase in the form of wisdom, knowledge and understanding. The disciple must have a constant diet of the word of God coupled with praise and worship, prayer and fasting. Once the diet is implemented and sustained, the carnal man will starve and the spirit man will gain strength.

The disciple cannot expect to grow spiritually strong while feeding the soul with the things of this world. Some Christians spend several hours each day watching programs on television that stimulate the soul while spending very little time in Bible study, prayer and worship. Many of these programs whet the appetite of the flesh and make the disciple spiritually dull. In other words, flesh gives birth to flesh and spirit gives birth to spirit. The person we feed the most is the person who will experience the most growth. So, who are you feeding? If we want to grow in the measure and stature Jesus grew in, we must do the things Jesus did. His life was one of intense dedication and devotion to His heavenly Father. Every disciple must have the same devotion and dedication concerning the kingdom of heaven. There is nothing intrinsically wrong with television, movies or other mediums of entertainment; we just need to be aware of what we are allowing in our ears and eyes as they also are entering our spirit. I personally feel there is an anti-Christ spirit in Hollywood because the image that is projected is not one of spirituality but carnality.

God created man with a God-consciousness. The Scripture reveals that a man God created was a tri-partite being, which means, man is made up of body, soul and spirit. Man is both a material being (body) and an immaterial being (soul and spirit). In other words, the body represents the unconscious existence, the soul represents the conscious existence and the spirit represents the God-conscious existence (Bere, 2011). The soul of man is made up of three parts: intellect, will and emotion. This is clearly the conscious where man reasons, makes decisions and feels. *"And the LORD formed man of the dust of the ground, and breathed into his nostrils the breath of life; and man became a living soul" Genesis 2:7(KJV).*

The breath of God allowed man to come alive intellectually, emotionally and in His will. God did not blow breath into man for him to act and live independently of God. Man was created to commune with God in the third realm or the third dimension of glory. Sin caused man to be separated from God and with separation came death. Jesus offers redemption through His blood so we can have fellowship with God in the third dimension. We were not redeemed to be part of a religious denomination, but to be prepared to dwell perpetually in God's presence, which is the third dimension. Once we get the revelation of why we were created and why God gave something as precious as the blood of Jesus for our redemption; we must commit ourselves to Him.

WHEN A DISCIPLE OPERATES IN FULL COMPLIANCE WITH GOD, HIS THREE PARTS (BODY, SOUL AND SPIRIT), WILL BE IN TOTAL UNITY AND BALANCE LIKE THE GOD HEAD; THE THREE WILL OPERATE AS ONE. ONCE THE THREE IS OPERATING AS ONE IN GOD, THE THIRD DIMENSION OF GOD'S GLORY WILL MANIFEST IN AND THROUGH THE DISCIPLE LIKE BRILLIANT DIAMOND.

The God Head had to come down to the tower of Babel being built by the unified people. God is trying to take us to a place where we can come up to Him. Anytime God deals with man He has to condescend by coming down; He desires to bring man up to the third dimension. In order to bring man up, God's word came down and the word formed man. In *Exodus 19,* we see a picture of God's plan to prepare a people for the third dimension of His glory. In the third month after the Israelites were brought out of the bondage of Egypt, God brought them through the wilderness to purge and cleanse them so they could come before His presence. Moses was told to *"sanctify the people today and tomorrow, and let them wash their clothes, and be ready against the third day."*

The Hebrew word for sanctify is *qadash,* and it means to *make clean, to dedicate, to purify and to prepare.* In order to meet God our vessels must be cleansed and purified. This is the crux of the matter concerning our salvation. God did not bring us out of darkness into His marvelous light to sit in church buildings waiting for the rapture. Like the Israelites before us, he brought us out of bondage so He could cleanse and purify us to live in His presence or to have His presence living in us.

When Christ came into the world to offer His life as a ransom, he did it to prepare a people for divine habitation. Disciples with a third day or a third dimension revelation know that it is all about habitation and not visitation. We do not want Him to come and go; we want Him to take up residence in us. We understand that to be a dwelling place for Him our temples must go through the process of purging and purification by heat and pressure just like the heat and pressure applied to the mantle of the earth to form diamonds. Just as we refuse to settle for Cubic Zirconia, we should refuse to settle for anything less than to get to a place where we can dwell in the third dimension of His glory. For the freed slaves coming out of Egypt their clothes had to be washed, for the convert in Christ that is coming out of the world it is a washing through the blood of Jesus that appeases the wrath of God and a purging through heat and pressure that prepares them to be vessels of honor.

Chapter 12
The Solitary

When all is said and done, you will stand alone and stand strong!

A Solitaire Diamond is one that is set alone in a distinctive setting for the purpose of enhancement. Traditionally, the Solitaire Diamond is large and may appear to be by itself or it might be surrounded by smaller unobtrusive stones to accentuate it. A gemstone that is set as a solitaire is esthetically pleasing and captures the attention of the eye. Thus, when God sets an individual or a nation apart as a solitaire, He does not do it solely for esthetics or cosmetics, because His solitaire does not bring attention to itself, but radiates Glory that focuses the attention on Him. His solitaire is an example to those individuals or nations of the transformation that comes through obedience to His will. God uses His solitaire not to overshadow that which surrounds it but to lift them from where they are to a greater place in Him.

Random House, Webster's College Dictionary defines the word solitary as, "*without companions; sole; being the only one.* The Hebrew word for solitary comes from the root *yachad* (pronounced *yaw-khad*) and it means to be or become one, to join or to unite. With that definition in mind we understand that the solitary is not designed as a punishment, but as something to bring unity and togetherness. God processes and prepares the solitary individual and uses that individual to unite as one the previously fragmented and divided group. From the beginning of creation God used a solitaire. God's plan started as and has always been a family plan. When God created Adam He was a **solitary** placed in a beautiful Garden called Eden. The word Eden comes from a Hebrew word which means pleasure, delicate, or delight. Although he was placed in an idyllic environment, the Bible declares, *"And the Lord God said, It is not* *good that the man should be alone; I will make him an help meet for him" Genesis 2:18(KJV)*. As beautiful and peaceful as the garden was, there was nothing or no one to compliment Adam. Like the solitaire it stands alone for a while but is eventually accompanied by accent diamonds. When God spoke about a help meet, he meant a suitable helper, or a helper corresponding to Adam. It was at that moment that the institution of marriage was established. God created Eve to be with Adam and together they walked in spiritual unity and had dominion together. There was no need for headship or cause for the woman to be silent. God never intended for a man to dominate and rule over his wife or any other woman. Woman was not created to be subservient to man, his slave or a sex object, but to help man be fruitful. *"And God blessed them, saying, Be fruitful, and multiply, and fill the waters in the seas, and let fowl multiply in the earth" Genesis 1:22(KJV)*.

God's idea for blessings, fruitfulness, and multiplication is for a man and a woman to come together in holy matrimony, then work together as one unit. This is the reason why a homosexual marriage is an abomination and an aberration. This is the reason why that type of so called marriage cannot and will not receive the blessings of God, fruitfulness, and multiplication from Him. The homosexual couple may be the nicest people on the face of the earth, but once we step out of God's order for marital relationship, we lose His blessings. If that type of union was acceptable to God, then the male couple or female couple would be able to produce seed. Every seed has the ability to reproduce after its own kind. The seed in man's loins cannot be complimented by another man. When God told Adam and his wife Eve to be fruitful and multiply, He was instructing them to bring forth children. *"Lo, children are an heritage of the LORD: and the fruit of the womb is his reward"* Psalm 127:3(KJV).

When a born again believer takes a biblical stand for the sanctity of marriage as it is ordained by God, he or she should not be considered a bigot or homophobic. When the institution of marriage, as God ordained it, is upheld, a society will enjoy God's blessings; when the foundation is eroded, we see a disintegration of the moral fabric of society. I do not doubt that there is a correlation between the breakdown of the family unit and the various diseases plaguing our land. *"If my people, which are called by my name, shall humble themselves, and pray, and seek my face, and turn from their wicked ways; then will I hear from heaven, and will forgive their sin, and will heal their land" 2 Chronicles 7:14(KJV).* When we obey God's established order, we can expect blessings, fruitfulness, and multiplication, when we disobey, we can expect the opposite.

When Eve was deceived by the serpent and Adam transgressed, the ground that once brought fruitful blessings from God came under a curse. God did not curse Adam because He does not curse the person He has blessed. Adam's transgression caused his world to be cursed, and his fallen state caused the things he produced to be under that curse. When God told them to be fruitful and multiply, their obedience would have an impact on the creatures in the sea and on earth. In the same manner their disobedience has had a negative effect on all living creatures. *"Because the creature itself also shall be delivered from the bondage of corruption into the glorious liberty of the children of God. For we know that the whole creation groaneth and travaileth in pain together until now. And not only they, but ourselves also, which have the firstfruits of the Spirit, even we ourselves groan within ourselves, waiting for the adoption, to wit, the redemption of our body" Romans 8:21-23(KJV).*

When tragedy occurs, some people will say, "Why did God allow this to happen to me?" When Adam and his wife brought forth a man child named Cain, the curse of sin manifested itself when he killed his brother Abel. Cain's act of fratricide loosed a spirit of homicide in the earth that has been a strong man over the earth ever since. When inquiring minds desire to know why God allows certain tragic things to happen, the answer is, SIN. Sin entered the world through Adam's transgression, and through sin, came death and destruction. All of creation is under the bondage of corruption because, *"all have sinned and come short of the glory of God" Romans 3:23(KJV).* The question should not be, "why does God allow it to happen?" The question should be, "When will man realize there will not be fruitfulness and blessings from God for the families of the earth until he comes into alignment and obedience to God's word?"

I thank God that He is a God of forgiveness and restoration. His righteousness demands that sinners be judged, but He judges in love and mercy. When sin reached levels in the earth that demanded God's judgment, he allowed Noah, his family and two of every kind of animal to escape the flood by entering into an ark. He did it because of His grace. *"But Noah found grace in the eyes of the Lord" Genesis 6:8(KJV)*. Whatever state you find yourself in at the present time, you can find grace in the eyes of the LORD. Do not allow any demonic voice to tell you the state you are in or your condition is so wretched it is beyond His grace. Paul said, *"But where sin abounded, grace did much more abound" Romans 5:20(KJV)*. God's grace and His mercy towards us can never run out. Isn't it wonderful that the seat upon which He sits is called the mercy seat? Moses was instructed to make the mercy seat out of pure Gold, meaning His mercy emanates from a place of purity. Men are always trying to drag us before a judgment seat, but the seat of Almighty Yahweh is a mercy seat, Hallelujah!!!

Noah and his family found grace and were able to replenish the earth, but after a while men's sin began to permeate the earth again. In His mercy and wisdom God decided He would not destroy the earth again with a flood. Instead of destroying the sinful people of the earth God had a plan to restore and bless them. In order to activate His plan of redemption and restoration for creation, God chose a **solitary** from a family in Ur of the Chaldees. When God called him his name was Abram, which means, exalted father. God's plan for his life would mean a name change from Abram to Abraham, which means, father of a multitude. God promised Abraham that all the families of the earth would be blessed through him and through his seed. God's work is primarily done in the earth through a seed.

After the fall of Adam and Eve God told the serpent that the woman's seed would bruise his head. Fruit cannot be produced unless there is seed. When the Word became flesh and dwelt among the early believers in the form of the Lord Jesus Christ, the door was opened for all the families of the earth to be blessed by having access to God the Father through His Son Jesus Christ. Truly, the greatest blessing a family can receive is to have access to God with all the amenities and privileges a relationship with Him brings. Sin caused God's creation to be barren and unfruitful. It caused the land to be dry and the enemy of death to come upon man. Jesus Christ is the seed God planted in Mary's womb to break the chains which held us bound, and caused our lives to be fruitless. When Jesus Christ the Seed is not planted in the heart of an individual, he will be rebellious and his dwelling place will be a dry land.

It only takes one seed to produce a fruit bearing tree or plant with a plethora of other seeds. One sperm out swam thousands of others to fertilize the egg that gave us life, but in the life of the male or female, there are thousands upon thousands of other sperms and eggs. The patriarch Abraham was set in the earth as a faith seed or a **solitary** through whom the gentiles could be loosed from the chain of sin which held them captive. Out of Abraham's loins came the promised seed Isaac. Out of Isaac's loins came Jacob, and through his seed came a nation called the twelve tribes of Israel. God told the prophet Jeremiah, *"At the same time, saith the LORD, will I be the God of all the families of Israel, and they shall be my people" Jeremiah 31:1(KJV).* God chose the nation of Israel as the apple of His eyes, to be His people. He did this so He could bring forth the Messiah out of His people to bring the gentile families into a covenant relationship with Him.

It is awesome when you think of the fact that God set aside the man Abraham to accomplish this feat. That God would condescend to use a man for such a great task is mind boggling. It is just another example of His grace, mercy and love. All of mankind should have received a sentence of death because of sin, but instead of death God decided to provide eternal life for us. Abraham was not that man, but he was the **solitary** vessel used by God to bring the man into the earth realm. Great men have come through the annals of history, but none of them, no matter how many followers they had, could deal with the sin issue which caused man to be separated from God. Mohammed could not do it; neither could Buddha, Confucius, nor Krishna.

There was not a man in all the earth through whom God could repair the breach or build the hedge brought about by Adam. *He that diggeth a pit shall fall into it; and whoso breaketh an hedge, a serpent shall bite him" Ecclesiastes 10:8(KJV)*. Adam's rebellion created a pit that all human beings fell into. The pit of His rebellion caused the hedge to be broken, and the serpent to bite us. When God allowed the hedge around Job to be broken the serpent bit him. The only antidote for the poisonous bite of the serpent is the blood of Jesus Christ the Lamb of God. Through the ages, men have tried to appease the serpent's bite through various forms of religious and non-religious practices, but all to no avail. *"For the life of the flesh is in the blood: and I have given it to you upon the altar to make atonement for your souls: for it is the blood that maketh an atonement for the soul" Leviticus 17:11(KJV)*.

There is not one human on the face of this planet who can claim to be born without sin. Actually, a person might be crazy enough to make the claim, but the evidence of sin will be in their life. Believers in Christ know the word of God to be true, so we understand what Paul meant when he stated. *"For as in Adam all die, even so in Christ shall all be made alive" 1 Corinthians 15:22(KJV)*. Every living human and animal on this planet received life through the blood that runs through their bodies. Whether we realize it or not, we are connected through the same blood line. When the Apostle Paul saw the idolatry in the city of Athens, his spirit was stirred in him. He told the people that, *"God has made of one blood all nations of men for to dwell on all the face of the earth, and has determined the times before appointed, and the bounds of their habitation" Acts 17:26(KJV)*. Black men, white men, red men, and yellow men are all connected through one blood. To restore the families of the earth back to Him, God's plan was to use a man, but the man could not come from the line of Adam because of contamination. The seed would come from a woman but the nature would be God's perfect nature.

Through the Prophet Ezekiel the LORD declared, *"And I sought for a man among them, that should make up the hedge, and stand in the gap before me for the land, that I should not destroy it: but I found none" Ezekiel 22:30(KJV)*. There was no man in the earth qualified to stand in the gap or make up the hedge so God the Word became a man. *"And the Word was made flesh, and dwelt among us, (and we beheld his glory, the glory as of the only begotten of the Father,) full of grace and truth" John 1:14(KJV).* For the first time in human history the glory of God was embodied in a human vessel, not any human vessel, but a vessel specially prepared by Him; he was indeed a **solitary**.

The amazing thing is, God is still preparing vessels through Jesus Christ to carry His glory in the earth. God's desire as expressed to Abraham is that all the families of the earth experience this blessing. Search the scriptures and you will see many instances where salvation did not come to just an individual but the whole household. Joshua declared, *"but as for me and my house, we will serve the LORD" Joshua 24:15(KJV).* When God thundered into the Philippian jail because of the prayer and praise of his sons Paul and Silas, the jailer wanted to kill himself because he thought the prisoners had escaped. Paul assured him that all the prisoners were accounted for. The jailer responded by asking Paul and Silas what he had to do to be saved. *"And they said, believe on the Lord Jesus Christ, and thou shalt be saved, and thy house. And they spake unto him the word of the Lord, and to all that were in his house" Acts 16:31-32(KJV).* What beautiful illustrations of God's plan, not only to save an individual but to bring salvation to the whole family.

The jailer and his household received salvation because Paul and Silas were set as a **solitary** in the Jail. They were severely beaten and placed in an inner prison with their feet fastened with stocks. Instead of lamenting their condition and the wretched environment they found themselves in, they chose to respond with prayer and praise. When they chose the option of prayer and praise, the Bible declares, *"the prisoners heard them"* Acts 16:25(KJV). Paul and Silas flowed in the spirit of *yachad;* they became one in prayer and praise and their unity elicited a response from heaven in the form of a great earthquake which shook the foundations of the prison. All prison doors were opened and all the bands were loosed from the prisoners.

God is sovereign and He orders the steps of the righteous. For His purpose and His glory He will set His servants in desolate places so His plan of salvation can be fulfilled. God's plan was not only for the jailer and His family, but the prisoners also. God is not going to open prison doors to release unregenerate criminals back into society to wreak havoc. I believe beyond a shadow of a doubt that the bands were loosed off the minds of those prisoners, and then the physical bands were loosed. Paul and Silas had every reason to fall into a state of despair and depression, but they chose to look beyond their circumstance and situation, and adopted a posture of prayer and praise.

So much of western Christianity is based around the individual prospering. Many of the sermons coming over the television and radio sound more like speeches from charismatic motivational speakers, telling us how blessed and prosperous we will be financially. We do not hear many sermons on suffering for righteousness sake, or forsaking all for the gospel of the kingdom of God. God's plan is that His kingdom will be established and His will be done in the earth as it is in heaven. When the kingdom of God is established in the earth realm, individuals and families will prosper. We must endeavor to get away from an individualistic social gospel that ties prophecy to monetary gains. We must adopt the mind of the Lord Jesus Christ so the plan of God can be established in the earth; His plan is for the covenant blessings He promised Abraham to come to the families of the earth. Our God is a God of covenant.

The blessing of Abraham is the Holy Spirit of God coming upon the Gentiles. Without the Holy Spirit Gentiles are consumed and controlled by perverse spirits. God desires to pour out His Spirit on all flesh. Jesus told His disciples, *"Nevertheless I tell you the truth; it is expedient for you that I go away: for if I go not away, the Comforter will not come unto you; but if I depart, I will send him unto you. And when he is come, he will reprove the world of sin, and of righteousness, and of judgment" John 16:7-8(KJV).* Forty days after His resurrection and ten days after His ascension, the promise of the Father that was given to the patriarch Abraham for the families of the earth came upon the believers tarrying in the upper room.

The promise came on the day of Pentecost and on that day Peter stood up with the eleven to deliver the New Testament Churches' first Holy Ghost sermon, he told his listeners, *"For the promise is unto you, and to your children, and to all that are afar off, even as many as the Lord our God shall call" Acts 2:39(KJV).*

The promise of the Holy Spirit is a gift God has provided for every one willing to call on the name of Jesus for salvation. A believer need not beg, sweat or plead for the Holy Spirit, because He is a gift promised to us by the Almighty God. If you are a believer with unsaved family members, stop worrying and start invoking the covenant blessings of Abraham and the promise of Pentecost over them. Our Father in heaven is a promise keeper not a promise breaker. Abraham's blessing and the promise mentioned on the day of Pentecost belongs to all believers because of the finished work of the Lord Jesus Christ. When He hung on the cross, He declared, *"It is finished"* What was finished? His work to redeem mankind and open the door for the blessing God promised through Abraham to come upon the families of the earth. Is not your family part of the families of the earth? Well claim the promise for them.

You may not have been born in to a wealthy family, a royal family, or an educated family, but God set you as a solitary in your family to bring out those bound with chains. Your parents may not have been married when you were conceived. You may have come into this world with some type of physical defect, but God has set you in place as a solitary so through you He can pour out His spirit on the people you come in contact with. You may not feel like you have what it takes in terms of ability, but God is not looking for ability He is looking for availability. When we avail ourselves to Him, and allow Him to set us apart through a process of sanctification and consecration, He will elevate us above measure and use us in a mighty way.

When Paul was chosen on the Damascus road to bring the gospel to the heathen; he described the experience by saying, *"But when it pleased God, who separated me from my mother's womb, and called me by his grace, To reveal his Son in me, that I might preach him among the heathen; immediately I conferred not with flesh and blood: Neither went I up to Jerusalem to them which were apostles before me; but I went into Arabia, and returned again unto Damascus. Then after three years I went up to Jerusalem to see Peter, and abode with him fifteen days. But other of the apostles saw I none, save James the Lord's brother" Galatians 1: 15-19(KJV).*

God sets the chosen vessel in a solitary place to prepare them for the suffering they will endure for the gospel. The solitary place is not an easy place to be, because we are designed for contact. Remember what God said concerning Adam, He said it was not good for him to be alone. The solitary is set apart by God for a time and a season, because God does not want any distractions during the process of preparation. If you are in a lonely solitary place to-day, in the furnace of affliction, remember the three Hebrew boys. They were thrown in to a fiery furnace but when the king looked in he saw a fourth man and He had the countenance of the Son of God. The Lord Jesus Christ is in the fire with you and the only thing that will be burned is the things that were holding you back from your destiny in Him.

It has to be extremely difficult to leave all that is familiar to embark on a journey through strange lands to fulfill God's plan and purpose. God was preparing Abram to be the father of all who would come to know Him by grace through faith in the Lord Jesus Christ, so He had to separate Him from his comfort zone. Our comfort zone can be an ungodly zone. We develop soul ties to people, places, and things. God takes us into the solitary place to renew our minds, and to give us an understanding of His will. There are individuals in a solitary place because they have lost a spouse through divorce or death, some are there because they committed a crime that has landed them in prison for many years, if not a life time, some are there because of some sickness or infirmity. Whatever the case or the situations, use what appears to be a stumbling block to be a stepping stone. When you experience a setback, don't take a step back, because God is working on your comeback.

Psalm 68:6 (KJV) gives us a beautiful picture and encapsulates God's reason for setting the solitary in families. The psalmist wrote, *"God setteth the solitary in families: he bringeth out those which are bound with chains: but the rebellious dwell in a dry land."* God sets the solitary in families so He can use them to deliver others who are bound with chains. He does this so the spirit of rebellion can be destroyed, and they which once dwelt in a dry land, can enjoy the showers of His blessings.

FROM THE WORD SOLITARY WE GET THE WORD SOLITAIRE, WHICH IS NOT ONLY A CARD GAME BUT A PRECIOUS GEM STONE; A DIAMOND. WE ADMIRE DIAMONDS FOR THEIR ESTHETICAL BEAUTY BUT A DIAMOND IS TOUGH ENOUGH TO CUT STEEL.

This process gives the individual the toughness and sturdiness need to cut steel chains, so the captives can be set free. The beautiful glistening solitaire diamond we see in the window of the jewelry store did not start out like that. The believer we see glistening and radiating the glory of God did not start out like that. Like the diamond in the window, the believer in Christ has to go through extreme heat and pressure in order to shine. There are many examples in the scriptures of individuals who endured the heat and the pressure in preparation for their divine assignment. You, the reader, can tell your own story or stories of the hardships you have had to endure for your divine kingdom assignment. There can be no conscientious objectors amongst believers who have a calling from God on their lives.

The level of heat and pressure we experience is correlated to the level of our assignment in God. Chains have various levels of thickness which represent the level of bondage God will use us to break. In order to break the chain the solitary individual has to be at a certain level in God. To get to the necessary level, there must be commensurate heat and pressure. Joseph was called to preserve posterity not only for his own family, but the families of Egypt and the surrounding nations. In preparation for his assignment God set him as a *solitary* by allowing him to be betrayed by his brothers, lied on by Potiphar's wife, and forgotten by the baker.

Some of the greatest attacks we will endure will be from friends, family, and people sitting in the church with us. Have you ever suffered betrayal at the hand of a friend, a family member, a spouse or someone in church? That type of betrayal is extremely difficult to deal with because it comes from someone you trust, and it usually comes at you when your guard is down. God calls us to spend time in a solitary or lonely place in preparation for the backlash we will suffer when he calls us to be His mouthpiece. Moses spent forty years traveling the deserts of Midian; David spent time living in the wilderness in caves and had to encourage himself in the Lord when the people he helped picked up stones to stone him. Jesus spent forty days and forty nights in the wilderness alone in preparation for His public ministry.

Some people have been abandoned by their spouses, rejected by family members, and wounded by leaders and lay members in the local church. The betrayal has caused many to retreat into a place of melancholy and depression. Many have left one church with the baggage of betrayal on their backs as they try to assimilate into the order of the new church. Many have gone on to new relationships with the old baggage of betrayal with them. Sooner or later the hurt and the pain of the unresolved situation will rear its ugly head, if there is no deliverance. When you get to the place where you are overwhelmed by the solitary place and the process you are going through, just surrender your will to God and ask Him to allow His will to be done. Just imagine for a moment, how difficult the place and the process was for Jesus. He had to be tough enough to break the chains of every family member of the earth who needed deliverance from sin. He had to go through a process with enough heat and pressure to prepare him to fulfill His divine assignment.

You have been set apart by God as a solitary but before you can carry His glory in the earth, before you can be His chain cutting tool, you will have to pass His test. You will not have a testimony until the test is passed because God does not believe in promoting us if we are not able to pass His exam. The solitary place is not your final destination. It is your class room, the place God prepares you for graduation into your calling. If the calling of God on our lives was not great, our test would not be great. Do not be overwhelmed by your current test. Open your eyes and envision the glory which shall be revealed in you through this test. Discern what God is trying to teach you, and who He wants you to reach and learn to give Him thanks for His will being done in your life. ***His ultimate goal for you is that Christ be formed in you, that you become the solitaire precious diamond He can use to bring out those bound with chains.***

www.ingramcontent.com/pod-product-compliance
Lightning Source LLC
Chambersburg PA
CBHW021336090426
42742CB00008B/629